# These *Wings* Can *fly*

## DISCOVER THE POWER OF YOUR MIND

## VIVIENNE DUKE

Grosvenor House
Publishing Limited

This book is published by
Grosvenor House Publishing Ltd
28-30 High Street, Guildford, Surrey, GU1 3EL.
www.grosvenorhousepublishing.co.uk

A CIP record for this book
is available from the British Library

ISBN 978-1-78148-863-8

This book is dedicated to my precious family.
Jon, Ben, Livia and my mum and dad.

# Contents

# FOREWORD

*"There are only two ways to live life*
*One is as though nothing is a miracle*
*The other is as though everything is"*
*ALBERT EINSTEIN*

This is the story of two ordinary people who travelled quite an unexpected and extraordinary journey together. Whilst they each took different paths, they both made the same discoveries and together, they began to understand the amazing power that rests within every one of us.

During this journey, travelled by me and my husband, this power was awakened and I would like to share our story with you in the hope that it will have the same amazing impact on your life that it did on ours.

I have learned so much over the last few months that has helped me through probably the most challenging time of my life and I want to share this with you because I know today's world is a pretty tough place to live for most of us. In the face of adversity, where I honestly could have crumbled (and I have had so many people saying, "I don't know how you are dealing with this." that I almost started believing them!!!) I have come out the other side having grown as an individual with a newfound courage and self- esteem that I thought had been permanently bashed out of me. I am often heard to say, 'What doesn't kill you makes you stronger." and this is so true. I also have an absolute clarity on my future and an excitement that I know who I really am and what my life purpose is - which is going to make me incredibly fulfilled and happy from hereon in (and already is!).

My aim with this book is to condense some of the key things I have learned during some quite amazing experiences and avid self-study over the last two years and try to make it accessible to everyone. There are so many books out there about self-help and don't get me wrong, they are brilliant and have certainly helped me enormously, but sometimes I think it is good to hear it in the story of an ordinary person that you can relate to and see some parallels with your own life.

I have not become a millionaire because of my discoveries, but I have certainly become richer and abundant in terms of my health; my self-esteem; my happiness; my hope and my courage to deal with challenging people and situations. I have also attracted a load of wonderful people into my life and existing friendships and relationships have gone up another level massively. People have come back into my life that were only mere acquaintances a year ago and we have developed incredibly strong bonds as they have joined me on my journey. I have never felt so supported, loved and fulfilled in my life.

This foreword is really quite important because it sets the scene for the rest of the book and also for some massive shifts that I believe are going on in this world today.

At the moment – these shifts are all still a little bit 'behind closed doors' and yet they are definitely going on because I have seen it for myself over the last two years and it has been pretty profound. It is actually blurring the boundaries between what is regarded as ordinary and what is regarded as extraordinary and I find myself now talking almost a different language. Words that a while ago I would have thought were the ramblings of someone who was slightly 'loopy', yet I now find that perfectly sane people are responding to me in the same language!

Without fail – whenever I have told anybody about my experiences – it has been like a light has switched on for them. Believe me – it has taken a bit of courage to tell people my story because it isn't your ordinary everyday situation, but I was strongly compelled to take this risk (in fact it felt like I would be failing if I didn't do it!) and not once has anyone ridiculed me. In fact – quite the opposite – it has enabled them to open up about their own experiences and I have had many people say, "You have explained a mystery that I have been living with for a long time."

Let me introduce myself. I am a pretty ordinary, down-to-earth Yorkshire person. Born in Leeds, England (still live there now) into a wonderful (but pretty ordinary) family and had a very secure, happy childhood and felt much loved. We were – and still are – a very close family. Nothing really extraordinary to report on my childhood – I was regarded as pretty intelligent (an A/B grade type student) – I was the middle child of three, with two lovely brothers. We fought, like all siblings do, but pretty rarely and we were incredibly close as kids and did lots together. We still do lots together now, albeit we are all a little older and the next generation has now appeared. We have seven kids between us (the average 2.4 children) all now teenagers. We all live in Yorkshire and see a lot of each other.

I am blissfully married to the most wonderful man and have been for nearly twenty five years. We have two lovely children who have done us proud. Our son is at University and our daughter is preparing for her first set of 'big' exams at school.

I have worked since I was sixteen and had a pretty successful career in a bank for seventeen years, following which, I left to set up my own business. I have been my own boss now for over fourteen years in the field of equality and inclusion and have had a varied and stimulating career. I have had my fair share of challenges, including riding out the UK recession and adapting the business to meet new needs, but in the main it has been the best decision I ever made and has given me the freedom to do what I really want to do.

Having had a pretty carefree and happy, contented life, the last few years have been probably the most challenging in my life and there have been many occasions when I have been heard to say, "Why me?" I now realise there was a very important reason why these challenges presented themselves in my path – so I could grow as a person, have a clear vision of where I am going and to lead a rich and fulfilled life.

This is my journey and quest to find my true self and life purpose – and it is told to you as a story. I will be baring my soul because I feel it is important to share this story with as many people as possible to give them hope and excitement for their life ahead. I almost see it as a film with me as the main character and – as with all good films – there is a brilliant cast who have supported (and tested!) me along the way.

I sincerely hope that my story inspires you towards seeking a greater understanding of yourself and gives you a 'map' to reflect back on your own journey so far (and what you have learned from it) and some directions for following your own journey of self-discovery.

I am so proud of how I have come through in the face of adversity and the experience has given me courage to face any challenge that life puts my way. I sincerely hope this book helps many people - that is my intention - and if you feel you are going through things in your life that seem almost unbearable right now please know there is always a light at the end of the tunnel. My inner light now shines very big and very brightly.

## How this Book works

My journey began with a quite unexpected 'spiritual' occurrence. It came as a surprise to me (because I have never been particularly spiritual) and in seeking to find some answers I found myself in this amazing world of discovery where the 'spiritual' converged with the 'science' time and time again.

I'm a pretty down to earth person so I did question things along the way and found that I was getting scientific proof for a lot of things I had never fully understood and always regarded as a bit 'out there'.

My husband, Jon, has been at my side throughout. He is about as down-to earth as they come and will not believe anything unless he sees it with his own eyes. There was a time when he did genuinely struggle with the experiences I was having, but as I moved through the journey of discovery and learned more and more about the 'science' of the power of the mind, Jon began to understand and even embrace a lot of the things I was learning and experiencing. He began to see how much of these 'self-help' tools and techniques were already applied in the business world (they were just diluted a bit with business speak).

He read some of the books I was reading and really began his own journey alongside me. I was still pretty much sticking to the 'spiritual' approach because my first experience had been so profound. Jon stuck mainly to the 'science' approach and we found a point of convergence that suited us both.

So – this book has turned into the story of two people, with two different perspectives, sharing the same journey. I am hoping this offers you a unique and varied read.

Jon will feature in the book with his own take on things (The View from the Ground) and how he walked slightly behind me to start (watching my back), then alongside me and then found his own path of self-discovery, which ran parallel to mine. Our relationship has certainly gone up many levels by us treading this journey alongside each other. Vivienne

## View from the Ground

If you have got this far through the foreword, it is hopefully because you have invested in a book that I believe will truly interest and inspire you in equal measures, rather than you are having a cheeky read in the local book shop.

Let's get something straight, when Vivienne (or as I like to call her - Viv) talks about me understanding the science, what she means is that I have come at this subject from a very black and white point of view. If I can see it and understand it, then I will feel it. If I can feel it, then I will live it and love it. Sounds strange? I hope as I interject through Viv's story, this will become a littler clearer.

As Viv has said, I am down–to–earth, or a better expression would be grounded. I like beer (but drink wine); eat Indian food too often; watch rugby league; attend the Leeds Festival every year with our son and am addicted to Facebook.

Viv has explained how I have followed her on this journey. All I would ask is that you read this book with an open mind and an open heart, and I promise you will be really inspired.

I am inspired every day and am proud to be married to Viv. She is my inspiration and I believe you will understand why as you 'fly' through the pages - a pun intended - in the spirit (sorry, there's another one) of the book. We talk every day about the positive influences on our lives and that is a massive shift from only 12 months ago when, if you heard us, you would have thought we had nothing. The fact of the matter is, we had everything, we just were too blinkered to realise it.

This is genuinely a magnificent read. How can I be so sure? I've lived and breathed it and I can absolutely say every day is now brilliant. Every day brings something positive and believe me, coming from someone who used to mourn at finishing over half of his glass of wine that is a revelation.

Read on and be inspired or if you are in the local book shop, wander over to the shop assistant, smile and proclaim you would like to invest in this book.

**Jon**

Jon will feature in the book with his own take on things (The View from the Ground) and how he walked slightly behind me to start (watching my back), then alongside me and then found his own path of self-discovery, which ran parallel to mine. Our relationship has certainly gone up many levels by us treading this journey alongside each other. Vivienne

## View from the Ground

If you have got this far through the foreword, it is hopefully because you have invested in a book that I believe will truly interest and inspire you in equal measures, rather than you are having a cheeky read in the local book shop.

Let's get something straight, when Vivienne (or as I like to call her - Viv) talks about me understanding the science, what she means is that I have come at this subject from a very black and white point of view. If I can see it and understand it, then I will feel it. If I can feel it, then I will live it and love it. Sounds strange? I hope as I interject through Viv's story, this will become a littler clearer.

As Viv has said, I am down–to–earth, or a better expression would be grounded. I like beer (but drink wine); eat Indian food too often; watch rugby league; attend the Leeds Festival every year with our son and am addicted to Facebook.

Viv has explained how I have followed her on this journey. All I would ask is that you read this book with an open mind and an open heart, and I promise you will be really inspired.

I am inspired every day and am proud to be married to Viv. She is my inspiration and I believe you will understand why as you 'fly' through the pages - a pun intended - in

## How this Book works

My journey began with a quite unexpected 'spiritual' occurrence. It came as a surprise to me (because I have never been particularly spiritual) and in seeking to find some answers I found myself in this amazing world of discovery where the 'spiritual' converged with the 'science' time and time again.

I'm a pretty down to earth person so I did question things along the way and found that I was getting scientific proof for a lot of things I had never fully understood and always regarded as a bit 'out there'.

My husband, Jon, has been at my side throughout. He is about as down-to earth as they come and will not believe anything unless he sees it with his own eyes. There was a time when he did genuinely struggle with the experiences I was having, but as I moved through the journey of discovery and learned more and more about the 'science' of the power of the mind, Jon began to understand and even embrace a lot of the things I was learning and experiencing. He began to see how much of these 'self-help' tools and techniques were already applied in the business world (they were just diluted a bit with business speak).

He read some of the books I was reading and really began his own journey alongside me. I was still pretty much sticking to the 'spiritual' approach because my first experience had been so profound. Jon stuck mainly to the 'science' approach and we found a point of convergence that suited us both.

So – this book has turned into the story of two people, with two different perspectives, sharing the same journey. I am hoping this offers you a unique and varied read.

the spirit (sorry, there's another one) of the book. We talk every day about the positive influences on our lives and that is a massive shift from only 12 months ago when, if you heard us, you would have thought we had nothing. The fact of the matter is, we had everything, we just were too blinkered to realise it.

This is genuinely a magnificent read. How can I be so sure? I've lived and breathed it and I can absolutely say every day is now brilliant. Every day brings something positive and believe me, coming from someone who used to mourn at finishing over half of his glass of wine that is a revelation.

Read on and be inspired or if you are in the local book shop, wander over to the shop assistant, smile and proclaim you would like to invest in this book.

**Jon**

# ACKNOWLEDGEMENTS

I have so many people to thank for their love and support during the creation of this book. Not only have they been constant supporters and cheerleaders of the book but they have also given me all the love and strength I needed to get through some pretty challenging times before and during the time it was being written.

For his constant love and support I want to thank my husband and soul mate Jon. Not only did you encourage me along the way but you also turned into my co-author and transformed this book into something pretty unique and special with your humorous 'view from the ground'.

My precious children Ben and Livia who have always helped me to understand what true unconditional love means.

To my mum for being my mum. I am so lucky to have you as my mum and the safe haven of your home and hugs where all my challenges just seemed to melt away.

To my dad for being a great dad. I miss you but I know your parting from this world opened up a whole new world for me.

To my wonderful friends who have all contributed so much to my personal development over the last two years and also became my willing proof readers when the book was completed: Kathy Wood, Jean Garrod, Anj Handa, Amanda Heenan. Thankyou my angels.

To Ryan Askew who came into my life recently and I believe for a very important reason. To give me the courage to write and publish this story and to talk openly about my experiences despite them being a little 'unusual'! It has been such an honour and blessing to feel I have inspired you with my story.

To Amanda Heenan for the wonderful cover design painted after reading some of the book.

To Steve Ramsden and Caroline Sheerin for reading the completed book and giving me such positive feedback. Your lovely, heartfelt words have helped to propel me forward in getting the book published and out in the public domain.

Finally I would like to thank the person that instigated the biggest and most positive personal shift that I have ever had in my life. He is referred to in this book as the X Man and without him keeping up the momentum of challenge, I would not be in the happiest and healthiest place that I am today.

# The Flock

*"Friends are as companions on a journey, who ought to aid each other to persevere in the road to a happier life."*
PYTHAGORAS

Here's a quick overview of the wonderful characters in my story.
Jon – my husband
Ben – my son
Livia – my daughter
Mum – my mum
Dad – my dad
Kathy – my best mate
Jean – my mentor and guide
Amanda – the purest person I know
Bruce – my older brother
Anj – my friend and business associate
Ryan – the window cleaner
The X Man – a main character in my film who could be seen as the 'baddy' but who actually got me started on the path to self-discovery and unbeknownst to him, has kept up the challenge and momentum which has propelled me forward. Thankyou.

# CHAPTER 1

## The Journey Begins

*"The only journey is the one within"*
RAINER MARIA RILKE

*"The journey of a thousand miles begins with one step"*
LAO TZU

2012 was a challenging year for me – probably the most challenging one I had experienced in my life.

My business was being impacted by the UK recession and we had to downsize in terms of our operations as business was reducing.

My personal income was slipping quite dramatically as a result.

A key supplier had received some bad press which we had to communicate and manage with our clients.

The X Man was proving to be the most challenging person I had ever worked with in my life. Not only directly – but also his impact on other people, which I had to deal with as they all turned to me.

My self-esteem was being battered beyond all recognition. I was subjected to criticism and sometimes aggression, almost daily, and I was beginning to feel like I was pretty useless at everything.

I was experiencing all the physical signs of extreme stress and anxiety. Tight chest, pounding heart, and constant lump in my throat and at its worst I had a few panic attacks, which are the scariest phenomena to handle.

On top of all these challenges at work, my dad's health was in serious decline. He was in and out of hospital which was putting an enormous pressure and worry on the family. We were all incredibly concerned for our mum's health as this was being impacted by the daily stresses of caring for my dad.

Looking back on it now, I realise I was wallowing in self-pity and could not understand why all these 'bad' things were happening to me. After all – I was a good person – wasn't I? I had never done anything bad in my life, I had always tried to be good to people, so why was I being punished with all these bad things in my life? Everything seemed to be spiralling out of control on a downward journey and I was getting pretty close to breaking point.

One week in September, I had experienced a particularly bad time. My dad had been rushed into hospital and we were told to be prepared for the worst. He was dying and the hospital had said that, given his age (he had reached the ripe old age of 85 bless him), he would not be a candidate for any kind of resuscitation if he slipped away. The family were devastated and we drew ourselves in to support each other, particularly mum (who was probably dealing with it better than any of us).

On one particular day that week I had been subject to a ferocious attack from the X Man. I had actually thrown the phone across the floor – I just could not believe how cruel he was being to me given everything that was going on with my dad.

Mum and I visited the hospital that evening and dad was quite lucid. He had made a bit of a recovery and as a family we were all clinging on to any little improvement he made. He kept asking me to talk to the doctors to find out if he was going to be OK. A lovely, kind doctor took me into a private room and reiterated that, whilst dad was making a slight improvement, he had serious heart failure and we still had to be prepared for the worst. He advised that they would not recommend resuscitation if dad's heart stopped as the procedure could actually do more damage to dad because it is so invasive.

I had to walk out of that room with a smile on my face to go back to my mum and dad with some encouraging words. It is one of the hardest things I have ever had to do – but dad looked so hopeful and expectant I had to lie to him.

On the way home, mum turned to me and said, "Now tell me what the doctors really said." to which I just burst into tears.

That night I got home and went to my sanctuary, the bathroom. Ever since my children were babies, this had been the one place where I could just slip away from the realities of the world for a few moments and have a bit of 'me' time. I sank into the bath, put my head in my hands and said imploringly;

"WHY IS THIS HAPPENING TO ME!!!!!!!!"

I was rather shocked and surprised to receive an audible answer. Without even thinking, I entered into a dialogue with this voice and here is how it went.

VOICE: "Because you are being tested."

ME: "Why am I being tested?"

VOICE: "Because you have to be strong."

ME: "Why do I have to be strong?"

VOICE: "Because you have an important role."

ME: "What is my role?" I must say at this point, I did actually think I might have actually tipped over the edge (you know what they say about talking to yourself and getting an answer back!), but the voice was so strong and clear it could not be my imagination and I felt compelled to carry on this 'conversation'. I also genuinely did not feel like I was thinking up the answers in my head (like when you sometimes give yourself a good talking to). There was also a strong feeling that I was being told something incredibly important and life changing.

VOICE: "To help people get on with each other." This didn't feel like me just being sociable with people and stopping them arguing. This felt like it was a job on a much bigger scale.

ME: "But how will I help everyone to get on with each other?"

VOICE: "Kathy will explain." Kathy is my best buddy - a pretty down to earth Yorkshire person like me.

ME: "What about the X Man?" – I felt I had to ask this because I was seriously wondering if I still wanted to be around this guy.

VOICE: "He is a lost soul, but you can save him."

ME: "Do I have to??!!!" – you can see I am quite getting into the flow of this conversation!

VOICE: "No. It's your choice but he can help you with your role."

ME: "What about Jon?"

VOICE: "He will keep you grounded."

ME: "Are you God?" – I'm a pretty inquisitive person and I wanted to know who I was talking to!

VOICE: "No – I'm an angel."

I'm hoping this next part shows my lighter side and also that I am quite an opportunist and that I did still have all my faculties about me. Here I am talking to an angel – I'm going to think of as many questions as I can that I want answering!

ME: "Will I ever be rich?"

ANGEL: Silence

I'm now thinking, "Stupid!!!! What did you go and ask that for when you are talking to a pure angel?" But I still couldn't stop myself.

ME: "Will I at least get my kitchen diner extension?"

ANGEL: "Yes" – I almost felt this was said with a bit of a raised eyebrow!

I then, quite tangibly, felt the presence move away and there I was - sat in the bath - thinking, "Did that just happen to me – or have I really gone bonkers?"

I kept thinking about the conversation over the next few days and the more I over-thought it, the more I rationalised it away as me just being in a state of extreme stress and hearing voices. But my intuition was still telling me that something pretty profound and special had happened to me that night.

Then, on 10 September my dad passed away and my world changed forever.

---

## View from the Ground

My role here is meant to explain the 'science'. At this stage, there is no science – just pure, brutal emotion. This was a truly horrendous time for Viv and for the family as a whole. No person should experience the external challenges that Viv was facing, particularly at a very hard emotional time for her.

Of course, I was worried for her throughout this period of time and her health (and to be honest her mental state) were a concern. So, with that in mind, I can fully understand if you have a slightly raised eye brow after you have read about a discussion with an Angel in our bathroom.

However, I must emphasise that Viv is a very straight forward person and therefore, for her to believe that this conversation took place, well, I needed to be there as support and not to question. Our magnificent relationship has been built over nearly 25 years of marriage on a solid foundation of love, trust, support, and belief in each other.

So, please, please, persevere because this story is real – you just need to read on.

**Jon**

---

## Kathy explains

*"Friendship is a single soul dwelling in two bodies"*
*ARISTOTLE*

*"A true friend never gets in your way unless you happen
to be going down"*
*ARNOLD H GLASOW*

Let me give you a quick low down on Kathy. She is like me - pretty down to earth. She has worked in office jobs most of her career, although recently she had trained as a reflexologist and was growing her own business in this area. I have loved seeing her grow and develop the business, doing something she is passionate about and she is a real inspiration to me.

One of her clients is my mum and Kathy used to regularly visit her at home, so she knew my mum and dad well.

Kathy has had her fair share of ups and downs over the last few years but has coped really well. I met her through our sons as they were in the same year at school. We moved in the same circle of 'mums' but never really got close, although there was something about her that I really liked despite not knowing her that well.

We were drawn together when she was going through a particularly hard time in her life and have remained the closest of friends since. She feels like my 'soul mate'. We are definitely on the same wavelength and we have some fabulous chats when we get together, including the more 'spiritual stuff' – even though neither of us had a particularly strong leaning that way. We have both always been of the view that there is something bigger out there and our latest 'putting the world to rights' conversation had been centred on the Mayan Prophecy (as we had all 'survived' 20th December 2012!) and the fact that the world was moving into a feminine era. We both liked the thought of this new era of 'girl power'!

The day after my dad passed away I was due to see Kathy, for one of our regular 'girlie nights', to do more putting the world to rights.

I texted Kathy to say I really didn't feel I would be much company and to cancel our get together. Kathy responded in her usual thoughtful way, "Hi Viv, I completely understand, but it might be good for you just to get out of the house. We can sit outside at the pub and I'll go in for drinks so you don't have to face people." It was just the little prompt I needed and I knew Kathy was right. Little did I know at the time that this would turn out to be one of the most important moments of my life.

We chatted for a while about dad and for some reason I suddenly remembered the 'bath experience' and what I had been told. I relayed it to Kathy including the bit about her 'explaining'. Bless her – Kathy looked a bit bemused and said, "I really don't think I can give you an explanation. Sorry hun, but leave it with me. I'll have a think and also speak to some people I know who may have the answers."

The next day Kathy rang me (which is unusual in itself because we are definitely 'texters' in how we communicate with each other when we are not sitting over a glass of wine together). She sounded quite excited.

KATHY: "Viv, I've spoken to someone about this and they said you are an earth angel."

ME: "What's an earth angel?"

KATHY: "I'm not entirely sure but the lady I spoke to said you are definitely an earth angel and you have been told what your life purpose is."

ME: "Wow! That sounds quite cool – I'll see if I can find anything on the internet."

I am the kind of person who thirsts for knowledge and if a small mystery is put my way – it lights the fire in me to find out as much as I can about the topic. I immediately got onto the internet, but didn't expect to find much as I thought it might be something that the 'hippy tree hugging' type people were into. Sorry to all those 'hippy tree hugging' type people. I now know where you are coming from and I think you are largely misunderstood and actually have got it right in terms of how you live your life! One of the big aims of me writing this book is to show that this isn't 'hippy tree hugging' stuff – it is something that absolutely every 'ordinary' person should seek to understand and embrace.

## Wings Unfold

*"Be who you are and say what you feel because those that mind don't matter and those that matter don't mind"*
*DR SEUSS*

I Googled 'earth angel'.

Wow! There is loads of stuff about this and the more I looked, the more I realised it was something that a huge number of people knew and talked about. There were perfectly ordinary people talking about this extraordinary phenomenon as though it was the most normal thing on earth.

I also discovered there are different types of earth angels depending on previous incarnations and what you have learned from past lives to bring to this one. There was even a quiz online that you could do and it told you what type of earth angel you are. I discovered I am a 'Mystic Angel' which is part 'wise one' and part 'incarnated angel'. So, I had already been on this earth and had been some kind of sorceress, witch or soothsayer. Ha – that made Jon smile! This intrigued me because I often joked with friends about us being 'white witches' when we had moments of 'coincidence'. I could also see people in my life very clearly in the 'earth angel' descriptions and I began to get this strong urge to tell them.

This was where I got a bit nervous because I thought, "Here you go Viv – you are exposing yourself to ridicule now. At best people will humour you but think you have gone slightly bonkers at worst they will say it to your face and probably avoid you from here on."

But there was something in me that was compelling me to do it – in fact I felt that I would be failing them if I didn't.

Talk about a challenge being presented to me. The first person I felt compelled to tell was the X Man! I had read a description for an earth angel called 'Star Person'. It was uncannily accurate in every way. "Hmmmm – so how do I broach this subject?" I said to myself. "I know!" I thought, "I'll just copy and paste the description of a Star Person into an email and send it to him saying "Does this sound like anyone you know?"

So that's what I did one evening. I figured that if he came back and said "No." then I would just drop it.

Next morning I got an email back from him saying "Do you mean like this?" and he had sent me the results of a quiz he had done which showed him being 100% Star Person and 0% human!

I replied back and said, "If you are interested to know how I came upon this and you have an open mind let me know and I'll tell you the story."

The X Man replied to say he had an open mind and would love to hear it.

So, I gathered my courage and called him. I basically chatted him through my bath experience, expecting a bit of ridicule at any point. When I had finished I sat back ready to take the barrage of jokes and the X Man said; "You've just explained something that has been a mystery to me all my life. Thank you. I now have a name for what I am and an explanation for why I am like I am. It has given me a lot of comfort to know I am not the only one."

Wow! That was not the reaction I was expecting but I felt so proud of myself that I had been brave enough to share what I had discovered and that it had had such a positive and profound effect on the one person I thought would be derisory about what I had to say.

I then thought of my friend Amanda. She is so pure and lovely, I just knew she was an Incarnated Angel. In fact – can you believe – whenever I described her to people – I used to say, "Amanda is like an angel." and a lot of other people described her in this way.

Amanda is a very deep and thoughtful person, but we had never had any kind of spiritual discussion – so again – I felt like I was exposing myself a bit, but had that same compulsion to tell her.

The conversation went pretty much exactly the same as with the X Man and Amanda almost word for word responded in the same way. "Thanks Viv, you have just explained a massive mystery to me – I am so grateful."

Next on my list was my brother Bruce. This one came about in a slightly more interesting way. There is an earth angel type called "Knight Paladin". I was convinced this was Bruce, given some of the things he has always been interested in since being a child (Samurai warriors, Masons) and was mulling over it one evening while in my car.

ME: "I wonder if Bruce is a Knight Paladin?" – (you know when I read back over this sentence it even sounds a bit bizarre to me!!!!).

BOOMING VOICE IN MY EAR: "YES!!!"

ME: "Should I tell him?"

BOOMING VOICE IN MY EAR: "YES!!"

ME: "What is his role?"

BOOMING VOICE IN MY EAR: "He is here to protect you."

ME: "Who are you?"

BOOMING VOICE IN MY EAR: "Michael"

I have since discovered that Michael is an Archangel and one of his key roles is to protect and guide people through the storms of change.

So, off I go again on my mission of communication. Now, I felt like I was exposing myself quite a bit. This was family. This was the man I had grown up with – my big brother – who teased me quite a bit when I was younger, but who was also a pretty sensitive 'gentle giant' and did indeed protect me quite a bit during my daft teenage years. So the same story got rolled out to my brother.

I got exactly the same response – "You have just explained a real mystery to me." I then said "I was told what your role is." To which Bruce got a bit emotional and said "I know what it is." Then in unison we said, "To protect you/me."

I think you will probably guess that, by now, I have been pretty much convinced that something quite big is going on in my world and that things are shifting fundamentally in terms of my own spiritual journey.

Another term I saw which was used a lot in relation to 'earth angels' was 'light worker', which basically means someone who is on this earth to carry out an important role in terms of the development of humanity and the universe. I actually now believe that we are all 'light workers', it is just that some of us have 'seen the light' a little ahead of others.

I must also point out at this stage that Jon was doing a very good job of keeping me 'grounded'. He is a very 'ordinary' chap and he was struggling a bit. He really wanted to believe what was happening to me and the experiences I was having, but was struggling because he had no experience to draw on and has never been a particularly spiritual person. I do think at some point he probably did get quite concerned for my sanity and I know he was keeping a very close and loving eye on me.

He admitted that he is the kind of person who needs to see something for his own eyes to believe it – and I respected that. I suspect that most people on this planet are like that but I am definitely seeing a shift in consciousness and what I realised is there are various angles that you can come at this from.

## View from the Ground

My experience of angels was Charlie's Angels on TV; the Robbie Williams song and pictures on Christmas cards.

So, this stage of Viv's developing story was a challenge for me at the time, although I was relieved to be told that I had been assigned the role of the 'grounded one'. It would take a hurricane to get me off the ground, as I am of a rather 'solid' build (or as our daughter says, cuddly, with squishy shoulders).

However, it is essential to emphasise that the most important person in this was Viv and she truly believed that she had had these visitations and discussions with an Angel. That in itself provided her with incredible comfort and belief, and that in turn made me realise there must be something in what she was saying and seeing.

Through that, I started to listen intently and slowly the interest began to take hold.

**Jon**

## Previous Flying Experience?

*"I know that there is a reason for everything. Perhaps at the moment that an event occurs we have neither the insight nor the foresights to comprehend the reason, but with time and patience it will come to light"*
DR BRIAN WEISS (psychiatrist and bestselling author)

Those that are close to me will tell you that I had a bit of a tussle with myself in terms of including this part of my story.

It is so personal to me and family members, but I kept getting a gentle and persistent nudge from those 'higher' voices that I have learnt to listen to. I also realised, having written other chapters in the book, that this story is really quite important in understanding every aspect that affects our minds.

One night, a few weeks after my dad's death, I had been round at mum's house. I go round there every Tuesday night and she makes tea for me. This routine started when my kids were young and it was mum's lovely way of giving me a little break once a week. It has become a really important part of my week - even more so when we were all gathering in as a family to support each other after dad died.

My mum is the most wonderful person. I feel blessed to be her daughter and everyone loves her. We spend most of our time putting the world to rights (have you noticed I quite like putting the world to rights!) and had been doing this that evening. Mum was slowly getting used to life without dad and was being incredibly strong and brave. She mentioned that she might start tidying some of his clothes out and I advised her to leave it for a little while and to make sure one of us was with her when she did it. We carried on talking about other things and I eventually left to go back home in my car.

I was day dreaming a bit on the way home – not really thinking about very much (I was concentrating on my driving though!) when suddenly I heard:

"Hello love." It was quite unmistakably my dad's voice and sounded like he was sitting next to me. So much so that I turned to look in the passenger seat.

I felt a whole wave of emotions but it also felt like the most normal thing in the world. So off I go again with one of my 'unusual' conversations.

ME: "Hi dad. How are you?"

DAD: "I'm fine love thanks – just resting. How are you?"

ME: "We're all fine. Missing you like mad but we are coping and supporting each other."

DAD: "How's your mum?"

ME: "She's doing really well. We are all looking after her. We were just talking tonight about maybe starting to clear some of your clothes out. Are you OK with that?"

DAD: "Yes, that was one of the reasons I got in touch with you. There are some things I need your mum to keep."

ME: "OK. Can you tell me what they are?"

DAD: "There's a tie with a logo on it, some cufflinks in a blue box and a hanky with some initials on it."

I might point out, that at this stage, I didn't really know what dad was referring to but amazingly I got a vision of each of the items. I didn't recognise any of them but they were quite distinctive – especially the cufflinks which looked quite old and had a pearly finish to them on the top. The hanky (or handkerchief to you non-Yorkshire folk) was white with a red embroidered logo on one corner. The tie was blue and striped with a white logo (although I couldn't really make it out).

ME: "OK dad. I'm not sure what these are but I'll have a chat with mum. Why do you want to keep the hanky?"

DAD: Sounding a little sheepish. "It's got sentimental value. It was my mum's."

Then I felt dad's presence shift away and I was left driving home, feeling a little like I had with my 'bath' experience.

When I got home, I quickly wrote the list down before I forgot and then went to tell Jon. I am sure Jon will have some 'views from the ground' on this one.

The next day, I went round to see mum and told her the story. She was over the moon that I had spoken to dad and that he was OK and said she would try to find the items. I was quite hopeful she would because this would be about as much proof that I could get, that I was indeed communing with the spirit world and wasn't actually going bonkers.

I am delighted to report that mum did indeed find all these items. They were things she didn't even know dad had and my vision had been so uncannily accurate that it actually made me cry when I saw them.

So from this time on I became the 'communication channel' for mum and dad. It was lovely and mum was able to be reassured that dad was OK.

The fascinating part of this story for me is that I actually got to communicate with dad whilst he was on his own journey, transitioning through the spirit world and people I have spoken to since have said that my experiences with what dad told me, very much stack up with stories about 'near death' experiences and also those of hypnotherapists who have taken people into past life regression.

So I will share this with you as it is truly amazing and has actually given me a lot of comfort as to what will happen to me when I leave this mortal coil.

Every time I went round on a Tuesday night mum would say to me, "Ask your dad where he is and if he is with anyone." I think she was a little concerned that he was on his own.

In the early weeks, dad kept telling me he was just resting and I used to get a really lovely 'visual' of this cosy dark room with a flickering fire light and that dad was sitting in this big cosy armchair.

On one occasion when mum had asked me if dad was with anyone, I asked him the question and he said, "I showed you last night." In a flash I remembered a dream I had had which felt like I was watching an old black and white film. It was set against this really bright white light and all our old relatives were playing on a bowling green and having a bit of fun together. When I asked dad where he was he replied, "You were seeing what I was seeing." So I began to understand that the visuals I was seeing were as if I was looking through dad's eyes.

Mum was getting a little impatient with dad just sitting in a chair resting every time I asked him, but this went on for a while. Then one day I asked dad where he was and here's the conversation:

DAD: "I'm on the plane"

I know this book is about flying, but this was not the flying kind of plane. This was in actual fact a 'plain'. I immediately got a visual of a kind of desert plain. The sort of scene you would see in a cowboy film. It was very bright and you couldn't really see where the ground ended and the sky started but it was definitely like a desert plain.

ME: "What are you doing there?"

DAD: "I'm deciding where I go"

ME: "Really! Do you get a choice where you go?"

DAD: "Yes, after you have rested, you get to choose where you are going to go next."

Things went quiet on the 'dad' front for a while and then out of the blue one day, when I was driving home from mum's I heard:

DAD: "Hi love. I'm here!!!" I have to say dad sounded really excited. His voice sounded stronger and he just sounded so full of vitality.

ME: "Ooh dad. I'm so pleased for you. Where are you?"

DAD: "I'm on the green."

At which point I got the most amazing visual. It was a golf green on top of a cliff, looking out to sea. Now that is my dad's idea of paradise!

What I have to say is that the colours were like colours I had never seen before. The grass was green and the sea was blue but I have never seen anything so vivid in my life. It really was stunning.

DAD: "And I'm really fit and young........and really good looking you know!!!!!"

He just sounded so happy it was wonderful.

Since then I have had very short communications with him but only at my instigation and he often sounded a bit distracted – like I had interrupted him whilst he was taking an important golf shot (cheeky thing!).

That tells me, he has found his heaven and is happy – God rest his soul.

You can possibly now see why I tussled with putting this part of my story in this book, but I have learned to follow my intuition and that little nagging voice in my head – so I hope you enjoyed reading this part of my journey and there is a strong reason for me telling you this.

The more I have read on this subject the more fascinating it has become and the more I found it crossed over with other things I was discovering about the amazing power of the mind. I will refer back to this throughout the book.

For now I would just ask that you keep an open mind on this one. What seemed to be emerging through my spiritual encounters and reading is that we have been here many times before. It seems that the memories of previous lifetimes are still in our subconscious and this can impact on our current lives, so I was fascinated by this concept and wanted to learn more.

I recently read the most amazing book which covers this in much more detail than I can do justice in this book. My wonderful friend, Jean, lent it to me and it is called 'Many Lives, Many Masters' by Dr Brian Weiss. It is about a psychiatrist who gives hypnotherapy to a patient who is suffering some major fears and anxieties, which seem pretty irrational and cannot be directly linked to anything that has happened in her life. On one particular occasion, when he is giving her hypnotherapy to regress her back to her childhood, he realises she is actually regressing further back into a past life. I will not say much more as I would not want to give too much of the story away, but all I will say is that, where other avenues have failed to heal her of her fears and phobias, her life improves immeasurably through this past life regression.

That got me sitting up and taking notice. Could some of my issues be from things in my subconscious from past lives?

Reading Dr Weiss's book actually helped me to put this new section in my book (this was another of my little 'nudges'). There were a couple of reasons for this. Firstly Dr Weiss is an eminent psychiatrist and he was putting his neck on the line a bit in his professional circles by writing about his experiences. His story resonated with me because he felt compelled to tell it, even though he feared ridicule. The second reason is that in some of the regressions, his patient actually dies and he is able to ask her questions about her experiences between lives. There were many parallels with what I had experienced communicating with dad as he went through his journey.

There is a much bigger picture here and my horizon of understanding began to expand.

---

## View from the Ground

I have a very high level of admiration for Viv including this – mainly because my advice was not to include it! But, it's not the first time in our near 25 years of marriage that Viv has defied me. I hate to say it, but each time Viv is proved correct and this is no exception.

I will be honest that when Viv talked to me about these experiences / conversations I was initially concerned as to her state of mind. But, not wanting to repeat myself,

Viv knows her own mind and I have absolute faith in her. When looking into the whites of Viv's eyes, I absolutely believed everything she was telling me, even though this was a million miles away from what I understood – at that time – to be normal.

These discussions certainly made our conversations at the local pub a lot more intriguing – and certainly a diversion from the world being against us. More on that to follow.

**Jon**

## Knowing Your Destination

*"Having a rough day? Place your hand over your heart.*
*Feel that? That's called PURPOSE.*
*You're alive for a reason. Don't give up."*
*UNKNOWN*

In some ways – I was lucky because I got to find out my destiny and life purpose pretty quickly and I was told very clearly what it was.

This was the starting point on my journey of self-discovery and I reckon is a pretty important place to start. If you don't know where you are heading, you are going to have quite a challenging journey and will possibly never get there.

I also strongly believe that we should all be happy in our lives and this is a pretty good starting point to discover what your destiny is.

I am now absolutely certain that we are all here for a reason and it is as a contributor to the advancement and development of planet earth and humanity. I believe we are all 'earth angels' or 'light workers' and our task is to find out what ignites our passion so we can throw our all into whatever we do and lead a rich and fulfilled life. Hopefully, this will naturally advance humanity and the world and I think we all have a critical part to play.

This quote from Oprah Winfrey just about says it all for me:

*"To fulfil the highest, most truthful expression of yourself*
*as a human being, ask yourself 'WHAT MAKES ME COME*
*ALIVE' – because what the world needs is people that*
*come alive"*

I almost use this as my daily mantra or 'reality check' on what I am doing at any given minute. Is this making me come alive?

YES – keep doing it and do more.

NO – stop doing it or change it because you are not on the right track

The secret is in finding out what it is you love to do. I started to think - What is it that ignites my passion? What is it that gets me leaping out of bed in the morning shouting "Yes – another great day ahead!!!!!" What job is out there that will make me so happy it won't feel like a job? Where are the people who make me feel happy, contented and completely blissful? Am I living my perfect day EVERY day?

Just by asking myself these questions I scarily realised that I was way off track in terms of my own happiness and life purpose. I was very passionate about equality and inclusion so why wasn't I feeling passionate about what I was doing on a daily basis. I certainly didn't feel like leaping out of bed in a morning. It was all I could do to summon the energy to drag myself out of bed and I was almost filled with a feeling of foreboding about the day ahead. I was definitely not in a working environment that made me happy and it smacked me well and truly in the face that this was because I was not with people who make me feel happy. In fact I was with someone who made me feel all the negative feelings you can possibly come up with and as a result, I was not living my perfect day every day (in fact any day!!!!!)

## WHO AM I?

*"I just woke up one day and decided I didn't want*
*to feel like that anymore, or ever again.*
*So I changed. Just like that"*
*Unknown*

It is only perhaps when we are under extreme pressure that we start to question ourselves and what we are doing.

There are a lot of books and resources out there to help and what came through as a common theme in all of them is that the starting point is knowing yourself. This might sound a bit simple but when you really get into the process of discovering who you really are it is quite profound. I couldn't remember the last time I had actually sat down and really thought about knowing myself. I was so wrapped up in the day to day stresses of what was going on, I had almost forgotten who I was!!! I was doing things just for a 'quiet life', I was allowing people to control me and I realised there was a lot happening around me that just completely went against all my values.

I realised that I just had to have a bit of 'me time' and really sit back and think who I was and what I really wanted. What was it that was going to make me feel happy and fulfilled and leap out of bed in the morning? What job would I be doing that didn't even feel like a job and who were the people I wanted to be around?

Another discovery is that it is critical to love yourself and this isn't being egotistical in any way. If you aren't going to love yourself – who else is! You really do have to love yourself and know very clearly what you have to offer this world because then you begin to raise your self-esteem and belief in what you can achieve.

I have discovered a number of things about myself which I now know were standing in the way of me progressing in life and being completely fulfilled and happy and the main issue was my self-esteem. I was quite shocked when I first learned this because I am outwardly a confident, extrovert person. Others who knew me were also shocked, which I think emphasises the importance of studying yourself as deeply as you can.

A cause and effect of my self-esteem issues was that I was blaming everything and everyone else for my circumstances. I began to realise that if I went through life with that mind set it was not going to get me very far because

I would never feel that I have control over my destiny. It is also a pretty negative way of thinking that will spiral downwards if left unchecked and this was happening to me. It is what some would call a 'self-fulfilling prophecy'.

There are a number of exercises I have done over the last few months which brought me to the realisation that I was in self-pity/victim mode and I could see how being in this mindset laid a path before me that was making me pretty unhappy. I was actually quite shocked at this realisation because I have always prided myself on being optimistic and positive – definitely a 'glass is half full' kind of a girl (especially if it's wine!). I had allowed external circumstances and people to chip away at that natural optimism and positivity and the negative results were very plain to see.

I realised I had to do something to halt this downward spiral in its tracks.

I began to look at ways I could 'get a grip'! I embarked on this next leg of my journey with a steely resolve that I was not going to let my life carry on in this way. I devoured every book, email, internet article, positive quote, positive song and guru advice that I could to help me in this quest. I was not going to let this beat me and I learned an awful lot of good stuff on the way which I share in this book.

There are loads of great exercises and programmes you can go through to really discover yourself. I have included some of them at the end of this Chapter. I have also discovered that it is an ongoing journey and I have committed to staying on this path throughout my life.

I began to realise that it was my core values that were really how I was 'hard wired' to live my life. I realised that I would never be happy if I was in a situation and with people that completely went against these values – because these values were a part of me and were not for turning!

I discovered that my values were empathy, compassion, trust, optimism, positivity, honesty and integrity. This confirmed to me, even more, that I was completely in the wrong place with the wrong people in terms of my work. I also began to understand my reactions and emotions in situations and that these were led by my values and beliefs. I was feeling uncomfortable in pretty much every situation that I had to face at work and it was because it was all going completely against my values.

Vulnerability was a big issue for me. I realised that my reactions were because I was feeling vulnerable in many situations. I was feeling vulnerable because I did not feel in control of the situation and felt powerless.

What was emerging for me was that I didn't like conflict situations and did anything to avoid them, so as a result, I was behaving very submissively. I have heard this called 'passive aggressive' and it is not the best way to respond to situations. In fact you end up 'reacting' rather than 'responding' in a considered manner.

Guilt was another big one for me. I realised that there were many situations where I felt guilty in life. This was not a good emotion to have because it almost put me into a 'win or lose' mentality as I felt in any situation that someone was the winner and someone was the loser. I have to say, the X Man is quite a controlling, manipulative person and he played on this. He knew which buttons to press to get his own way.

Rather than trying to work out a way where everyone was a winner (and this is called being assertive!), I was always putting myself in the other person's shoes and not considering myself. I realise this has actually held me back in a lot of situations but also been a key driver for my feelings of self-pity because my guilt in a lot of situations meant I always put others first but felt like I was making a sacrifice. What a martyr!

Low self-esteem and guilt were holding me back and I was surrounded by negativity which was rubbing off on me big style and I was overloaded with constant negative emotions. I will cover negative emotions in a bit more detail later in this book as I discovered some pretty amazing techniques to get rid of them – even whilst still in the same environment.

I had a choice. Did I carry on working in an environment and with people that quite clearly went against ALL my values, or did I take the courageous move and follow my heart and get myself pointed in the right direction for my life purpose?

It was about time I 'got a grip' and started taking responsibility for my own life and not letting others run it!

The first important step was to really reassure myself that I had got my 'destination' right. I did not want to make the same mistake I had made four years ago by following my head and not my heart. I needed to point myself towards the people and work that would make my heart sing and get me leaping out of bed in a morning and I am delighted to tell you that I am now in that place (and it happened so quickly once I was on track, it was almost mind blowing!).

My life purpose had already been given to me by 'angel intervention' and it definitely felt like something that sat well with all my values and what I loved doing. I got confirmation of this through the exercises I did and there were two in particular that were very simple and yet very powerful.

The first was to think of a time when I REALLY felt elated and that I had achieved something and then to go a bit deeper and consider why this made me feel a real sense of achievement. The things that came out for me were:

*I was passionate about what I was doing.
*I was really feeling it in my heart
*I really believed in myself and so did others
*I really wanted to prove I was doing the right thing to the non-believers
*I was working with fantastic people who shared my passion and values
*I had established great client relationships

This exercise provided me with the 'blueprint' for my perfect working life.

Secondly, I asked myself the question "What do I want?" The knack is to answer the question from the 'gut' and not overthink it. Write down the first thing that pops into your head and then become that annoying toddler and start asking "Why?" Do not let up on yourself until you can go no further, but try to do it quite quickly so you don't spend long pondering on each 'why'. This is how it turned out for me:

*What do I really want?* - £1m (I know....I'm not very creative! But watch what happened next).

*Why do I REALLY want what I want?* – So I can have financial freedom.

*Why do I REALLY want what I want?* – So I can pay off all my debts and have some money behind me.

*Why do I REALLY want what I want?* – So I can focus on my book and doing what I really want to do in my working life.

*Why do I REALLY want what I want?* – Because I love the idea of being able to help people to help themselves and also connect people together for the greater good of society.

*Why do I REALLY want what I want?* – Because I am passionate about people and love to feel I have contributed to everyone being happy and getting on with each other.

Wow. I had just confirmed in a few minutes what I was told my life purpose was and the blueprint for my work.

So I hope you can see – not everyone needs a celestial visitation to find out what their true destiny is.

I am also delighted to report I am now living by my values. Guilt has turned into empathy and compassion; low self-esteem has turned into courage to follow my heart; negativity has turned into optimism and positivity and I am now able to follow my life on a path of honesty and integrity.

## View from the Ground

Viv's assessment of this period of our life is embarrassingly accurate. When we reflect now on what we were like then it is unbelievable. We still live in the same wonderful house; we still drive the same cars; we still drink the same discount wine and we probably have less money now, but it is hard to recognise the people we were.

Why has this happened, why hasn't that happened, why can't that happen? It's raining; it's too dry; the price of wine has gone up – actually, the latter really is something to complain about!

In addition, the X Man occupied so much of our conversation. As much as I would have liked to intervene, I had to maintain a silence and just listen to the mental hell that Viv was experiencing. The X Man has some talents, but people skills could never be listed as one. Unfortunately, I did not help Viv's plight as I have never been short of an opinion and I am always right (except when as noted above). Ironically, on a social level, we had some good times with the X Man, but his attitude towards Viv had the potential to tip her over the edge.

This book not only explains how Viv avoided that happening during her hour of need but also how she will ensure no one ever affects her like that again.

Something had to happen, and Viv has discussed how she started to tackle what was the equivalent of an illness – 'negativititis'. Listening to Viv told me that, if I was to help her, then I would have to change too. This bit would be the hard bit – because of my natural propensity to look at things from a half empty perspective. In addition, my idea of self-help was to walk an extra mile, rather than pick up a book, read a website, or look at one of the many other methods that have become natural to me now. More on that as I follow up some of Viv's incredibly wise words, with my ground up view.

One part of my change was to understand the deeper me. I wear my heart on my sleeve, but what does that actually mean? So, I commenced on a journey of reading a lot of the same material as Viv and we also discussed things in great depth and that gave clarity. A massive shift was the realisation that this positive thinking was .......... positive and natural, and life changing – if you want it to be. It's not weird. It's not the stuff of smiling faced door knockers, or leaflet waving city centre stalkers. It's good!

This was the start of an interesting process and what has turned out to involve life changing adjustments. As I have said above, more will be said on these adjustments later, but I am so grateful to whatever force it was that guided me to follow Viv. Our remarkably strong marriage and partnership has grown even stronger.

It will all become clear.

**Jon**

---

**Some exercises to find out who you are and what your true 'heart' destiny is.**

Think of three times when you really properly lost it. Describe the situation in as much detail as you can including how you reacted and why you reacted in that way

Think of three life changing moments. Describe the situation in as much detail as you can including why they felt like they were life changing and how you felt about yourself in these situations

Analyse your responses to the above two questions and try to summarise your findings in terms of:

*what situations prompt strong reaction in you – both good and bad?
*what situations make you feel vulnerable?
*how you want to be seen by others?
*how you think others see you?

Write down three people that you admire. Include in some detail what they are like, what it is about them that you admire and the impact they have on people around them. What you write about these people actually reflects the 'inner you'. This is how you are hard wired to succeed.

Write down three times when you have felt elated, invincible and on top of the world. Include how you felt when you were in these situations. The answers you give represent where you feel most at peace.

Think of three times when you really felt like you achieved something. What was it that ignited the flame? You will probably find some common themes come out here. This is really the 'blue print' for your perfect life.

Another useful exercise to go through (if you dare!!) is ask other people what they think about you. Sometimes you will find they know more about you than you do! This is a great exercise to also see if how you feel inwardly is how you appear outwardly. This was a really interesting exercise for me because a lot of people saw me as being really confident about what I do and they were amazed when I told them that two of my biggest challenges were low self-esteem and submissiveness. This also helped me to understand that often what you see in others is not necessarily what is going on inside. An outwardly confident, happy person could be in turmoil inside. This was certainly the case with me.

# CHAPTER 2

## Pointing in the Right Direction

*"I have learned that if one advances confidently in the direction
of his dreams and endeavours to live the life he has imagined,
he will meet with success, unexpected in common hours."*
*HENRY DAVID THOREAU*

My destiny was now very clear to me. I had also begun to learn how debilitating negative thoughts and emotions could be, not only on my peace of mind but on my physical health too. I quickly realised that I had to set off on this journey with the right mind set and I must therefore learn to take a bit of control over my mind which was presently running away with itself.

It was on this leg of my journey that I discovered some amazing things in relation to our minds and just quite how powerful they are. Not only does our mind have an immediate impact on mental and physical well-being; it has an impact on everything around us and actually creates our environment.

This might sound a bit far-fetched but this is a point where scientific and spiritual schools of thought really converge so I was absolutely determined to understand it and actually loved making all the connections between the spiritual experiences I was having and the discoveries and theories of the likes of Einstein.

This chapter has been the most challenging for me to write – mainly because when I first wrote it I quickly realised it was turning my story into an amateur scientist workbook and I am sure that is not what you really want. I experienced my first phenomenon of 'writers block'. I think that was someone telling me something! Some of my wonderful friends very gently, but firmly set me straight and advised me to continue with the discoveries through my own story.

There is a lot of this chapter that has ended up on the 'cutting room floor' because I realised that part of discovering the power of your mind is through your own research and discoveries and piecing it together in a way that you can understand. I also would not even try and replicate what quantum physicists and neuro-scientists have discovered through years and years of research.

So this chapter is going to be my 'layman's' take on what I have learned and I will just let you know what avenue I went down to make some of the discoveries I made.

What I have found is that the more I understood how my mind works, the better I got at harnessing its power and the more my life improved. I think that's a pretty good motivator to stick at something and try to understand it as much as possible.

Conversely, I found that in some moments where I let my commitment slip that things started turning wrong for me again, so I quickly found that this was something that really needed to become a part of my life.

I almost liken it to going on a diet. You follow it religiously but as soon as you come off the diet you put all the weight back on (and often more!). Or it could be likened to exercising your physical body and getting it in tip top condition but as soon as you take your foot off the pedal your fitness levels decline. All the experts tell us that diet and exercise must become a way of life.

I realised that the same has to be said for mastering your mind. It is such a precious and powerful thing that it can change your life in untold ways and I have seen it change my own life and the lives of people around me and those that I have read about and studied.

I started this journey with quite an unexpected spiritual experience but there are many other ways you can embark on your own journey.

My avid reading and study took me to varying sources of information including religious, scientific, psychological and spiritual. What I discovered is that whichever way you look at this (and feel most comfortable in accepting), everything points in the same direction and there is some powerful convergence in what I have studied.

I'm a person with a pretty open mind who likes a lot of variety – so I have found every angle fascinating and have loved making the connection between for example a religious view and a quantum physicist's view.

Another thing I have found very encouraging on my personal journey is that these different schools of thought are actually beginning to acknowledge the other viewpoints and as there is more and more evidence of the manifestations of the power of the mind – it is impossible to dispute it.

What I am attempting to do in this book is bring all that learning together in a format that hopefully will be accessible to everyone depending on which angle you feel most comfortable with.

Jon definitely felt more comfortable with the scientific angle and it was through this channel that he got on his own journey of self-discovery and also began to understand what I was experiencing.

# Miracles of Matter

Take That's song just about says it all. We are actually not solid. Every one of us is made up of a load of 'matter' or 'energy'.

In fact everything on earth and the Universe is made up of the same 'matter' it is just formed in different ways. We are actually 'ALL ONE'.

In terms of plants, animals and minerals – their matter is formed naturally and we call this nature. The form of these things changes by other natural forces including things like the seasons. Think about how the 'matter' of your garden or a local park changes throughout all the seasons.

Now humans are a little more interesting. We are not led so much by the forces of nature (although it does impact on us). We actually create our own environment through 'consciousness'. We were given the power of thinking to create the world around us.

The most fundamental thing I learnt through my studying is that our thoughts are 'energy' and actually form things in our lives if we give them enough power.

We are 'ALL ONE' so all our thoughts are part of one big Universal Mind.

Jon has put a bit of 'science' at the end of this section to hopefully summarise what I have just said here

It was a bit of a 'eureka' moment for me as I realised that I was a tiny part of a much bigger picture. Everything I was thinking and every emotion I was feeling was becoming part of the Universal Mind and would have an impact somewhere. The enormity of this really struck me. I began to see how all my negative thoughts and emotions were creating that environment around me. I was focussing so much on this negativity it was actually all manifesting in my life.

I then started to think about all the good things in my life and how I had manifested those and it was like a lightning bolt. The best part of my life was my family and friends and my beautiful home. How had these all manifested in my life? Because that was where I focussed all my positive thoughts and energy. I have a perfect relationship with Jon and that is because we are so 'in tune' with each other and give out positive energy (in the main!) to each other on a consistent basis. Our children are happy and settled and this is because they literally 'manifested' into a warm and loving environment.

What about all the negative things that had manifested in my life? I began to see clearly now that these were where I had focussed all my negative thoughts and energy and the manifestation was getting bigger and bigger because I was increasingly focussing negative thoughts (i.e. energy) on these things.

I had a sudden realisation that I couldn't go round blaming everyone else and every circumstance for the things in my life that I was not happy with. I had created them and therefore it was my job to sort them out and nobody else's!

And, I had to do this by getting my thinking straight.... literally!

## View from the Ground

As I have mentioned previously, I had started to read some of the books that Viv had studied, and I have noted below some of the things that I discovered.

Everything on this earth comes from one place, but there are different perspectives. Scientists appear to call this 'Source Energy'. However, many people call this God. There are others that call this the 'Thinking Source'.

Everything on this earth (including us!) is one great big lump of energy. Some of us more than others (sorry, I am conscious of my weight).

We are therefore all connected and we are all one (that does sound a bit out there but I think I have finally got my head round that one).

Human beings are just a big mass of energy (or, in the words of those wordsmiths Take That - 'miracles of matter') and so is every plant, animal, vegetable and mineral around us. I hope you are still with me.

Energy is moving in and out of form all the time. It moves into form and stays that way when it is 'observed'.

Humans consciously 'think' and 'observe' all of the time. Because of this we actually have quite a lot of creative powers. In fact we are co-creators with God (or the Thinking Source) and this is often referred to as the Universal Mind. Make sense?

Plants and animals are the purest form of creation because they just automatically rearrange energy and manifest form. There is not much thinking going on here and this is called 'nature'.

Our thoughts are energy – so when we observe our thoughts for long enough we actually begin to manifest them into solid form. We are therefore all the cause (or co-cause with other people's thoughts and God / Thinking Source) of everything around us.

Whatever we focus on and believe in our minds becomes a 'command' to the Universal Mind. These images manifest in our lives.

We are all part of one huge ocean of energy. We are all one. Any thought we have changes the Universe. We create a ripple around us which the Universe sends back to us multiplied.

I hope you are still with me and will continue to check in with my view from the ground later on. The above is just my observations on what I have read. To actually understand any of the above points, your local book shop or an on-line book website will be able to oblige with many books written by experts. I am just an interested person.

**Jon**

# Laws of the Universe

*"There is an orderliness in the Universe, there is an unalterable
law governing everything and every being that exists in our lives.
It is no blind law; for no blind law can govern
the conduct of living beings"*
*MAHATMA GANDHI*

It now felt like I was moving into a whole new realm of
knowledge. I realised that I needed to look at a much bigger
picture than just what was going on in my little world and as
I thought more and more about how it all pieced together in
the Universe – the answers started to appear in many of
the things I was reading (of course they did!!! – I was
focussing my thought energy on understanding the Universe
so the answers manifested in front of me!).

I started to read things on the Laws of the Universe. I never
really studied science much at school, so this was all new stuff
to me but I found it fascinating because it was resonating with
my life. I think the word 'Laws' is a good one because they
basically govern how everything operates in the Universe and
seen as we are all part of the Universe, I wanted to understand
how these Laws were going to impact on me.

I haven't detailed these Laws because there is so much
out there about them that it is easy to find information if
you would like to study it further. Probably the most widely
known one is the Law of Attraction. If you Google this you
will see what I mean.

Nature is a great way to look at the Laws of the Universe
in action. Humans don't have any control over nature
(although we are doing a pretty good job of trying to destroy

it!) and I began to look at things from a whole new perspective. The more I thought about it – the more I thought what a miracle everything is. I realised how much I just took for granted and it was like I was seeing everything with a fresh pair of eyes. It felt really good and actually started to subtly increase my levels of happiness and positivity (perhaps I am turning into a 'hippy tree hugger'!).

As I began to learn about the Laws – I could see very clearly how they were governing my life. But I was inadvertently harnessing most of them in the wrong way. The Universal Laws will always be in play and I felt like I had made a very important discovery that was going to add to all the tools I was using, to turn my life around and get myself back on track.

What I was beginning to discover very clearly was that 'energy' is a fundamental part of our lives and I wanted to try and understand this a bit more.

I really did feel like I had lots of jigsaw pieces and I was getting closer to seeing the big picture so I could start to piece them all together. So my quest continued to find out more about 'energy' and this was really where things started falling into place for Jon.

## Energy!

This was the turning point for Jon, in terms of understanding what I was experiencing and believing it to be possible. I think you will have seen by now that up to this point he had struggled a bit to believe what I was telling him. He always said he believed that I believed, but because he hadn't experienced it and couldn't see it in front of him it was a real struggle to believe it himself.

In keeping with her role of 'explaining things' to me, my buddy Kathy lent me a book. It was when I started studying this book on the Law of Attraction that things started to really fall into place for me in terms of the absolute power of the mind and I also discovered a way I could explain things to Jon.

### TRANSMITTING AND RECEIVING

Because we are all just made up of a mass of energy we are effectively like a radio transmitter. We are constantly transmitting out and receiving energy and this can be anything ranging from positive to negative.

Energies that vibrate on the same frequency resonate with each other so like attracts like energy. Remember everything is 'energy – including humans and our thoughts.

If your thoughts and emotions are negative – you are giving out negative energy and this is the frequency you are 'tuned into' – you will get more of the same back.

Conversely, if your thoughts and emotions are positive – you are giving out a positive energy and will be 'tuned in' to get more of the same back.

To understand this I got Jon to think about when he tuned into a radio station or a TV channel. You tune into a certain frequency and expect to get the channel you have tuned into. If you tune into a 'horror channel' on TV you are going to get a horror movie. You wouldn't tune into a 'horror' channel if you wanted a 'Disney channel'.

This really helped me to begin to train my mind. I certainly didn't want any more negative people or situations in my life. I had quite enough to deal with thank you very much.

What I began to realise was that I was giving far too much energy to negative thoughts and because these thoughts were being powered by negative emotions of fear, anger, jealousy (and even hatred at some points!) they were being given even more negative energy. I was actually creating and manifesting more negative things in my life and I just hadn't seen it.

This was a major turning point in my life. I had finally grasped one of the secrets to mastering the power of my mind but, as I am sure you are thinking, I began to think "Yeah easier said than done!!" How can you try to keep positive thoughts going through your head consistently and fuel them with positive emotions when you are in a negative situation right now?

The first thing I had to remind myself was that I had actually created this situation for myself so I had to take responsibility for it. I mentioned earlier that I had been in a vicious circle of self-pity and playing the victim and blaming other people for my situation. It suddenly dawned on me that I had 'brought it all on myself' and not only that, but even worse, if I carried on thinking this way I was going to attract more things into my life that made me have feelings of self-pity and being a victim. It was like a massive wake up call for me and I had to give myself a real good talking to.

I was very clear that it was my thoughts and emotions that had created everything in my life. I realised I had to do a complete turnaround in how I was thinking and it was from that moment onwards that something shifted and my life started pointing in the right direction.

Now being the inquisitive kind of a person that I am – I needed to understand this whole energy thing a bit more.

How is it that we actually give off this different kind of energy?

How is it created and how does it connect our mind, body and external environment?

## ENERGY CENTRES

A couple of things got me on this track of understanding.

First of all Kathy gently nudged me to start doing meditation. To be honest, I was a little nervous about this. It makes me smile looking back at it now, but at the time I honestly thought I might be opening my mind up to all sorts of weird spirits! Given I seemed to be quite open to the spirit world I was actually avoiding doing anything that might open myself up anymore. I realise now that meditation is actually a very powerful technique for managing the energy of your mind and to be honest, in today's challenging world, is probably a critical technique for everyone to learn.

My friend, Jean, also lent me a book called 'Hands of Light' by Barbara Brennan (a former research scientist for NASA) who had made the links between some of her scientific work and a natural healing talent that had started to shine through her. I was relieved to read this book. I thought, "Phew, I'm not the only ordinary person who is having these spiritual experiences!" Then I became absolutely transfixed with it. I was entering a whole new world of knowledge and I loved it.

I began to really properly understand how the energy of our mind, emotions and body all connect. I also began to understand why I was so open to connecting with the spirit world and how I could actually harness this to help others.

So by now I was pretty clear that everything that exists in the Universe is energy and this is all vibrating at different rates.

I now discovered that physical matter and energy are just two forms of the same thing. If you think about this in relation to yourself – you have a physical body and you also have an 'energy' body. Your physical body is a mass of energy particles that are vibrating at quite a low and dense level so it can be seen by the human eye and feels relatively solid. However, you are so much bigger than this (that sounds good doesn't it). You are actually possibly up to 60 foot bigger than this when we also look at your 'energy' body. We all have a much faster and finer field of energy around us that vibrates at a much lighter level. Many people call this our 'aura'.

When energy is balanced well across our body we experience good health and conversely when it is imbalanced we experience ill health or 'dis-ease'.

It is our subconscious mind that powers our energy and emotion. Every thought and the emotion it carries produces a change in our physical body and our DNA.

This made me think about some emotions and the physical reaction it prompted in me. When I was embarrassed, I blushed; when I was happy I smiled; when I was angry my heart rate went up.

I began to realise that a lot of the physical symptoms I had been experiencing were all as a result of stress. So my mind was playing out all this negativity and not only was this creating a negative environment around me – it was also creating 'dis-ease' in my physical body. For years I had suffered from chronic neck and shoulder pain and no amount of massage or therapy was easing it up and now I knew why.

So – how is it that the mind; the physical body and the energy body all connect?

This is where I really began to see the lines blur between 'spiritual' and 'scientific' and there was a lot of convergence going on in terms of the things I was reading. Words such as 'aura' and 'chakra' that I thought were the realms of holistic therapies and 'tree huggers' were being mentioned in scientific books I was reading. Fascinating!

The mind is like the 'programmer' for your physical body and energy body.

We are all pretty familiar with our physical bodies, so perhaps the best way to explain our 'energy' bodies is to compare the two and show how they are linked.

*Your aura is the equivalent of your physical body
*Your life force energy (referred to as Ki, Chi, Qi, Spirit or Holy Ghost) is almost like your blood
*Your chakras are high energy points in your energy body and are equivalent to your brain and organs
*Your meridians are the energy equivalent to your veins and arteries and they carry the Ki/Chi (or whatever name you prefer to give it) all over the body

So, let's have a look at these in a bit more detail.

## Aura

If you are like me, I used to relate the word 'aura' to angels and the halo above their heads. I only thought about it in the 'religious' sense and have since learned that there is a scientific angle to this and our aura is simply a part us that most people cannot see because it vibrates at a much lighter, finer level than our physical body.

The aura isn't just on top of our heads. It completely surrounds our body and is present from birth to death. It expands and contracts dependant on our health, emotion and mental wellbeing and how comfortable you feel in your surroundings. Some auras can be huge and they range from 6ft to 60ft around our bodies.

So when you think about it – your aura is always going to be intermingling with other people's auras when they are in your proximity. I realised that I had unwittingly felt other people's auras. I remember being in a room where I just felt absolutely drawn to someone and couldn't stop watching them. Many call this 'charismatic'. These people usually had really high energy or just appeared so calm and serene. Their aura is healthy so it is big and therefore 'touches' a lot of other people's auras.

## Chakras

These are high energy spots. The word 'Chakra' means wheel or vortex and if you look at pictures of chakras they look like a spinning funnel with the narrow end near our bodies and the wider end opening out further away from our bodies.

There are seven main chakras and they all relate to parts of our body. They are the link between mind, spirit and body. There are also 20 minor chakras around our hands, feet and knees.

Healthy chakras vibrate evenly in a circular motion and I have actually seen this and demonstrated it to other people. My buddy Kathy (doing really well in her role as 'explainer') bought me a crystal pendant for Christmas. If you hold the pendant over your chakra points it actually starts spinning in a very regular motion. You can feel the force of the energy spinning it around (almost a bit like you had put it in the top of a mini tornado). It is quite phenomenal. If you are feeling a little sceptical about this all I can say is that Jon has seen this for his own eyes and was quite blown away by it. I'm sure he'll mention it in his commentary.

Chakras are an essential part of our body's energy because they are intimately linked to our physical health. When they are balanced and opened so is the corresponding part of our body. When they are blocked, damaged or partially closed then it will have a negative impact on our physical body.

I was really drawn to try and understand as much as I could about chakras and the link between our mind, emotions and body.

I began to see how certain deep rooted, negative emotions I had been experiencing were quite literally making me physically ill and as soon as I began to master my emotions the resulting physical benefits were quite astonishing and happened very quickly.

I learned so much from understanding how these 'energy centres' affect our mental and physical wellbeing that I have tried to summarise below what each of them means and how they link to our mind, emotions and body.

RED – Root (Base) Chakra – I HAVE

*Location – Base of spine
*Physical body link – adrenals, skeleton, skin, blood, large intestine, pelvis, hips, legs, feet
*Emotional/life link – grounding, survival, security, trust, physical body, home, job, nature, earth

ORANGE – Sacral Chakra - I FEEL

*Location – Navel
*Physical body link – reproductive system, lower digestive organs, kidney, prostate
*Emotional/life link – relationships, sexuality, appetite, sense of abundance and wellbeing

YELLOW – Solar Plexus Chakra – I CAN.

*Location – Just below ribs
*Physical body link – pancreas, muscles, liver, spleen, upper digestive system, intestine, bladder, middle back
*Emotional/life link – personal power, intellect, purpose, destiny, self-empowerment, self-esteem

GREEN – Heart Chakra – I LOVE

*Location – Heart
*Physical body link – circulation, heart, lungs, immune system, upper back, arms, hands,
*Emotional/life link – unconditional love of self and others, balance, unity, compassion, kindness

BLUE (TURQUOISE) – Throat Chakra – I SPEAK

*Location – Throat
*Physical body link – throat, ears, nose, mouth, teeth, neck, thyroid
*Emotional/life link – communication, self-expression, sound, wisdom, clarity, truth and purpose in our communications

INDIGO – Third Eye Chakra – I SEE

*Location – Centre of forehead
*Physical body link – brain, head, eyes, face
*Emotional/life link – sub-conscious/higher self, intuition, creative, vision, spiritual awareness, charisma

VIOLET (WHITE/GOLD) – Crown Chakra – I HAVE

*Location – Crown (top of head)
*Physical body link – whole body and nervous system
*Emotional/life link – enlightenment, knowledge, self-fulfilment, universal consciousness, inspiration

I have seen a real move towards more holistic treatment of physical illnesses and very much based around 'chakra healing'. There are also a lot of techniques you can learn to work on this yourself and I will cover some of these in the 'Flying Skills' chapter of this book. I have experienced them and the positive impact on my physical and mental well-being has been profound to say the least.

From a personal point of view, the main physical symptoms I have suffered from in the past were neck, shoulder and back ache (I had suffered this for about 10 years), poor digestive system, high blood pressure, panic attacks and I once had a horrendous bout of sinusitis. As you can see, I was in a bit of a mess!!

When I look back, I can directly correlate these physical symptoms to negative thoughts and emotions I had allowed to run unchecked.

At the time I developed sinusitis (which literally felt like my face was frozen with a metal plate in it) I was afraid to speak up on any issue I had with the X Man. There were many things I was allowing to happen which completely went against by core values. But because I couldn't speak up, I hated myself and the X Man. My throat and heart chakras were clearly blocked or depleted at this time and it manifested itself in the sinusitis and also a serious muscular problem with my neck and shoulders. He was a pain in the neck and I was literally carrying the weight of the world on my shoulders (and it felt like it!).

Because I wasn't speaking up for myself, I also began to lose my self-esteem and the X Man's persistent criticism and undermining behaviour was not helping matters. I was allowing things to happen that were not on track with my values and life purpose and I felt powerless. My solar plexus chakra was clearly not in a good state and this began to affect my digestive system. Because I was clearly not getting all the nutrition I needed this started to have a negative knock on effect on other parts of my body such as skin, hair and nails.

I have not particularly changed my lifestyle but in the time I have been mastering the power of my mind and adopting the 'flying skills' (covered in Chapter 6), I have lowered my heart rate, lowered my blood pressure and got rid of all the pain and tension in my neck and shoulder which I had been suffering for years. The neck and shoulder pain literally disappeared overnight because I 'put my mind to it' and focussed on the positive.

On top of this – my immune system must be in tip top condition – not the slightest sniffle for me for as long as I can remember and my digestive system has completely returned to full health with the positive knock on effect of healthy skin, hair and nails. I have been told by many people that I am positively glowing and not one panic attack in sight.

How about that for the power of the mind!

## Meridians

These are the channels that carry our life force (Ki/Chi etc) around our energy body. There are a number of techniques that are used to keep this life force flowing freely and you will probably have heard of some of them – but like me perhaps not fully understood why people use these therapies and what they did. Well hopefully I have now solved a little mystery for you.

Any of the following are designed to keep that life force flowing freely and release any blockages: Acupuncture; Acupressure; Reflexology; Bowen; EFT (Emotional Freedom Technique or Tapping); Reiki. You will also probably have heard of things like Yoga and Tai Chi which are exercises and body movements you can do to physically release any blockages.

There I was thinking this was all a bit of mumbo jumbo and now I have directly experienced the benefits.

A revelation for me has been Reiki which I will talk about later in the book because it has had such a profound impact on me and the people around me that I have almost become a bit evangelical about it. It really is a miracle!!

So, to summarise – every negative thought, word and action will have a negative effect on your aura and whole energy body, including your physical body. Conversely, positive thoughts, words and actions raise our vibrations and ensure a smooth flow of the life force through us.

When the life force is flowing freely we feel healthy, strong, fit and full of energy. When it is low and there are blockages we will feel weak, tired and listless and more vulnerable to illness and 'dis-ease'.

I have learned that it is absolutely, categorically our thoughts and emotions that affect everything in our physical bodies and our environment so the key challenge is to try to take some control over our thoughts and emotions and I began to focus on understanding how our conscious and subconscious minds work together.

---

## View from the Ground

As Viv has alluded to, this is where things started to fall into place. A bit of a light bulb moment which, as we are talking about energy, is more than appropriate?

Kathy had lent Viv the Law of Attraction book, and that was a fascinating read. As has been said, I need to see things to believe and understand them. The book explains how what you give out you get back. Not rocket science, but it started to make sense – when pieced together with what Viv was talking about. Simple stuff like, I smile at someone and they smile back (note: I haven't tried this yet on the London Underground); if you speak in a cheerful manner, the response you receive is similar; if you get out of bed in the morning with the attitude that you will have a good day, well, here's the magic – you have a damned better chance of having a good day.

Please understand here, before all of this, my natural position – particularly on a Monday morning – was to get out of bed knowing I would have a bad day. I was never disappointed, and this ensured those around me experienced a similarly bad day. At this stage, I would like to say ..................... deal with it! No, sorry, I mean I am genuinely sorry.

With the Law of Attraction in hand, and with Viv's guidance, positive energy given out has produced positive energy back and I love it.

---

I have waded through other books, and they have provided guidance to where we are today.

Now, Viv has also spoken about the gift of the crystal from Kathy. Yes, this really blew my mind, but it's not a joke. I was amazed to see this crystal hanging over my chakras – more on these in a minute – and spinning unaided. What is this all about? Energy!

I recommend that, if you truly want to open up to what you read and learn from this book, give it a go.

As for the chakras, Viv has discussed these in great, but straight forward, detail above, but an understanding of the chakras has helped me as I have developed a desire to use life's energy positively and learnt how to channel it so that I can maximise its force.

Keep going – this is fun.

**Jon**

## Conscious and Subconscious Mind

*"Whatever we plant in our subconscious mind and nourish with repetition and emotion will one day become a reality."*
*EARL NIGHTINGALE*

*"If The Holy Spirit can take over the subconscious with our consent and cooperation then we have almighty Power working at the basis of our lives then we can do anything we ought to do, go anywhere we ought to go and be anything we ought to be."*
*E. STANLEY JONES*

It has taken me quite a long time to get my head round this (pardon the pun) but I think I have finally grasped it and I will try to explain it as straightforwardly as possible.

The conscious mind is responsible for logic and rational thoughts and all actions that are performed while you are conscious.

The subconscious mind controls an enormous number of things. It controls all the functions of our body (good job we don't have to consciously remember to breathe or for our heart to beat!!) and it also automatically triggers feelings and emotions.

The analogy I have used to help me understand how they work together is that of a computer. The conscious mind is like the 'programmer' and the subconscious mind is like the 'hard drive' where everything gets stored.

The sub-conscious mind is way more powerful than your conscious mind. My reading taught me that it represents about 80% of your mind power so is something worth understanding. It stores all of your previous life experiences (and as I discovered, your 'past' life experiences), your memories, your beliefs, your skills and every situation you have been through and every image you have seen and the beliefs/emotions you have attached to them.

I rapidly discovered that by learning how to train and use my subconscious mind I would be able to control my behaviour, fix my belief system and get rid of unwanted emotions.

However, I also realised this is much easier said than done. I found myself getting into a bit of a pickle with all the techniques I was learning regarding how to reprogramme your subconscious mind because it is actually quite a challenge to do this. I discovered that a lot of the programmes I had in my subconscious were pretty deep rooted (they've been there for well over 40 years and that's just in this life!)

Here's a few of the key things I learned which will hopefully get you on the path to discover your amazing conscious and subconscious mind.

For most of our lives (apart from when we were very young) the conscious mind has been programming our subconscious mind. So every conscious thought we have had and the corresponding emotion or feeling is programmed in.

The subconscious mind basically runs your life. Whatever is in there will be referenced in every situation you face or thought you have. If you have already faced a similar situation, or had a similar thought, the subconscious mind will get to work referencing and giving you all the emotions that you felt in the previous situation. This is actually a safety mechanism and I guess harks back to caveman times. "Ooh a fierce animal coming towards me." = feel fear = run! However, interestingly in this same situation − if you were a hunter it would possibly go like this "Ooh a fierce animal coming towards me" = get excited about dinner = fight.

The subconscious mind has to accept everything that the conscious mind gives it − this made me start really thinking about the importance of my conscious thoughts. If

I was constantly mulling negative things over and over in my mind and replaying them with all the negative emotion I was feeling then this was getting further and further embedded in my subconscious and with each time – the related emotions would just get worse and worse – and they did! Looking back I realised in a lot of situations I was making a 'mountain out of a mole hill' because of all the related negative emotions I had programmed in.

At its worst it did actually get to the stage where all I had to do was think about the X Man and my heart would start thumping and I would have all the physical symptoms of fear. I couldn't believe I had let that happen to me – but I had.

I am really happy to report that this no longer happens and I have used a whole host of techniques to overcome this – but if you are in a similar situation – I hope this helps.

The other thing I learnt is that the subconscious mind doesn't differentiate between what is real and what is imaginary. If you are thinking something – it is real according to the subconscious mind. This is why I was feeling all the negative emotions and feelings whenever I thought about the X Man. Even though he wasn't there in front of me – my subconscious mind treated it as if he was. Now I also discovered that this 'science' was actually a good thing if harnessed properly. If you are thinking lovely positive thoughts then the subconscious mind will think you are experiencing them and will give you the related emotion. This was where I really began to see how much I could use my conscious mind 'positively' to start making myself feel better and also start reprogramming some good positive stuff into my subconscious.

I have learned a number of techniques and ways to master my thoughts and these are shared with you in Chapters 4 to 7 together with some of my personal experiences of applying these techniques including where I have slipped up a bit. I always think it is useful to hear about mistakes aswell, so that you can avoid them.

So, before I start with these techniques I would like to just go back to my story and move it on a little further where the seeds of improvement in my life were starting to spring forth as a result of applying my early learnings.

## View from the Ground

I hope you have enjoyed what you have read so far. It's been a journey and one that we are proud of. Interestingly, it's only still early stages for us and we learn and celebrate every day. In addition, many friends didn't even know we had needed to travel the journey that we have.

Realisation was the starting point and Viv, with the guidance of Kathy, commenced the process and I am honoured and blessed (sorry, I am being a bit serious here) that I was invited along. You might think, "You're her husband so you should expect to be involved," but remember, if I can't see it I won't believe it and Viv persevered in finding a way to show me.

So, we have moved from realising we were suffering from 'negativitis'; looking at energy, through the Law of Attraction, giving out good and getting back better; not allowing the behaviour of one person to overwhelm our lives; understanding our chakras and watching that crystal swing.

It's all good!

**Jon**

# CHAPTER 3

## Flying in Formation

*"Take the first step in faith. You don't have to
see the whole staircase.
Just take the first step."*
*DR MARTIN LUTHER KING JR..*

When I was a young girl I remember going on a boating holiday with my family on the Norfolk Broads. I will never forget being witness to the most amazing phenomena I could remember seeing in my short life. There was a field at the side of the river and in it were loads of geese. They were all standing perfectly silently looking up into the sky.

Then without warning they all flew up into the sky in absolute perfect formation. I can remember thinking it was 'magic'.

How did these birds know to gather together?

How did they know the time was right?

How did these birds all know to stand in the right position to set off?

How did they know which direction to set off in?

How did the leader know that they were the leader and how did the other birds know this?

Having studied the Laws of the Universe, I now know that this is an example of natural laws in all their glory. Something attracted them all together on that particular day in that particular location. Something pulled them in a certain direction and something created a leader who they all followed. Something made them fly in perfect formation with not one jostling for position or straying away from the flock.

They flew in complete synchronicity.

Remember we are all just energy and we attract things around us that have the same energy frequency. Those geese must have all been vibrating at the same frequency and it drew them together. They were probably also all feeling pretty chilly and needed to get off to sunnier climes!

Plants and animals are the purest form of creation because they just naturally rearrange energy and manifest form. There is not much thinking going on here and this is called 'nature'.

However, because humans consciously think and observe we are co-creators in the Universal Mind. We are not pulled by nature we can actually think consciously about what we want to do and what we want to manifest in our lives. We are the cause (or co-cause) of everything around us.

So thinking back to the 'geese' scenario – I realised that as I was beginning to 'consciously' think positively and focus on what I wanted (and not what I didn't want!) and my life was beginning to do a bit of a U turn.

I was getting very clear on where I wanted to be and when I should set off

I was getting very clear on the right direction I should be pointing in

I was very clear on my life purpose and the kind of people I wanted to be with

I was very clear on the timing (although I did get some strong messages to 'slow it down' and 'go with the flow' which as it turns out were very sensible!)

I then began to try and harness everything I had learned so far – including the Law of Attraction.

And then the magic started to happen and people and things started to manifest in my life!

# The Law of Attraction

*"Therefore, I tell you, whatever you ask for in prayer,*
*believe that you have received it and it will be yours"*
*JESUS*

The Law of Attraction is part of the Universal Law of Vibration and is perhaps the most widely talked about in terms of how we create our own lives.

There is a mass of information out there on the Law of Attraction and a whole industry has grown up around it. You will not find it too difficult to access some information on this.

Many self-help books on how to attract money, health and relationships are all based on this Law and one of the most popular and successful of our time is 'The Secret'.

My journey of discovery has always led me back to this Law. Whether I was studying the psychological, scientific, religious or spiritual angle – they all point towards the Law of Attraction. Here are some of the fundamental principles I have learned and these could almost be a summary of the previous chapters:

*Thinking about something means it will begin to manifest. We are all energy that forms itself into things. Our thoughts are also energy. Whatever we focus on and believe in our minds becomes a 'command' to the Universal Mind.

*We attract good or bad experiences based on our thoughts. The subconscious mind does not know the difference between something real we are experiencing and something we are imagining. Therefore, if we think about something for long enough the energy of the subconscious mind will begin to attract this into our life. If we are worrying about something negative that might happen, or something negative that has happened then we are likely to attract more of the same types of negative situation into our life. If we focus on something positive and charge this with positive emotion then we will attract positive things into our life.

*The more we focus on something the more likely it is to manifest. The stronger your vision of what you want to attract and the more you concentrate on it, the more likely it is to be created. Not all our thoughts will immediately manifest themselves (good job!) but the more you think about something and the more powerful your belief and emotions, the quicker and more powerfully it will manifest in your life.

*Trust your intuition rather than over-thinking things. The 'intuitive' part of your mind is the subconscious. This is also known as the 'higher self' and is the part of your mind that connects with the bigger Universal Mind. Therefore if you trust your intuition and follow your 'gut instinct' it is far more likely to be a better approach than relying on your conscious mind that might rationalise away all your great ideas. I have certainly learned to follow my intuition and from the moment I did, my life started to turn around in a positive way. I followed my intuition in writing this book. My rational mind was saying "No Viv, you've never written a book before. You can't do it!" but I trusted my intuition and here we are! I also found that I started getting signs that I should write a book and these got stronger and stronger. Only today, I was having a slight wobble in my confidence about this book and I turned the radio on and 'Story of My Life' by One Direction came on! I have also tapped into my subconscious in a more focussed way by using techniques such as meditation and brain wave entrainment. I have found this begins to really open up access to my subconscious and the 'light bulb' ideas just flow.

*To change things in your life you have to see them how you want them to be. Not as they are. This is a great one for those of us who are going through a bit of a difficult patch in our lives. It's human nature to mull over things in our minds and don't you find the more you think about something bad, the worse it seems to get. We end up blowing it out of all proportion. You are playing out a negative scenario over and over again in your mind like a film and your subconscious mind is programming it all in! I started playing out a positive film of my future in my mind and it really started to make a difference. It immediately uplifted me if I was feeling down and I can actually see some of the things I visualised have now materialised in my world. It really is amazing! I also started switching my thoughts to what I 'did' want rather than what I 'didn't' want. It's quite a simple technique but immediately changes the way you think about a situation.

*Your relationships with people are what you have created – Now this might be a bit of a hard one to stomach but, believe me, it is absolutely true. I will bring the X Man into this one. On the face of it, I did nothing wrong. I am a good person and I know one of my skills is relationship building. So how could I have possibly done anything wrong in terms of my relationship with the X Man? I have since learned that 'I brought most of it on myself' based on my reactions and emotions to things he did. That was actually quite a hard lesson to learn but as soon as I accepted this, my life began to turn around.

I began to wonder if I could start physically manifesting things in my life if I thought long and hard enough about them.

The first definitive experience of this was when I was out for a walk with Jon. I was telling him about the Law of Attraction and, as mentioned previously, it was the science bit that really got him to understand what was going on in my world.

For a while, before and after my dad died, I used to see white feathers in really random places. I was told this was a sign the angels were watching over me. This gave me a lot of comfort and I used to think quite a bit about seeing them.

The more I thought about this, the more they appeared and the more random the places. The best one was when I had been on the phone to someone and I went to put the phone back in its cradle and there was a white feather resting there. Without knowing it, I was harnessing all the Laws of Attraction. I kept visualising feathers, I associated them with positive emotions and I wanted to see more and more because it meant I was being watch over and protected. There was one day where I literally walked through a path of them whilst out on a walk – there is honestly no way there could be so many feathers creating a perfect pathway for a few metres!

So Jon and I are walking along and I am explaining to him about the Law of Attraction in quite an excited and passionate way as I felt like I had made this amazing discovery. It was a pretty windy day and just as I got to the part about feathers – a white feather whooshed up in front of us and literally did a merry dance as we walked along. It then landed on the floor a little way in front of us. Jon was gobsmacked!! It was so windy I was convinced it would blow away so I kept saying, "Please stay on the ground, please stay on the ground." Sure enough it did and when we finally reached it, the tip of it was attached to the path as if it was superglued – amazing!

We then had a few weeks of fun with this new concept. I visualised seeing a three leaf shamrock and that very day for some reason I went a different way on my walk and a big Carlsberg lorry went past me on quite a narrow road. Ever seen the Carlsberg logo? I was quite excited about this, so carried on the visualising. The next day I was driving on the motorway in a speed restricted area (the usual roadworks!). A white van pulled up alongside me and then overtook me. What was on the back of the van? A huge three leaf shamrock.

It was the middle of summer so I thought I would set an almost impossible challenge and imagined seeing a robin. I pictured it flying out in front of me along a hedgerow I walk past daily. That morning whilst shopping I went down the pet aisle to get my hamster some sawdust for his cage – as I bent to pick up the sawdust what did I see? A birdseed packet with a robin on it. What did I see the next day while out walking? You guessed it – a robin flew out in front of me along a hedgerow. What did I see the next day in my garden? 3 robins!

So you can have a bit of fun with this and if nothing else it gives you a few funny stories to tell, but what was becoming very apparent was that the more I practiced it the better I got at manifesting things.

Going back to the first walk with Jon and discussion about feathers. It felt like quite a profound moment because it felt like a 'light bulb' had gone on in his mind and he finally 'got it'.

When I got home, I went about my normal housewifely duties which included the dreaded ironing!! I set the ironing board up and went into auto-pilot to get myself through the chore. When all of a sudden. POW!!!!!!! This thought hit me in the head and it was so powerful, I almost felt like I had been hit in the head. In fact I think I heard the words audibly:

"People Help People"

Let me explain this a little. I am a trustee of a charity which supports disability sport for young people (they have nurtured some of the Paralympic athletes). Like most charities, attracting funding was always a challenge and they were seeking to enter into developing partnerships with the corporate world to try and get financial and volunteering support – but were a little nervous about this as they had no experience of engaging with big companies. I worked with a lot of companies who were keen to support their local communities and some gave employees paid volunteering time but struggled to capitalise this into their communities because they didn't know where to start. This had been niggling at me for some time. Two groups of people – both with a common goal but not connecting. I had begun to think there should be a service that enabled these connections.

We also need to bring into the mix a track I had listened to quite a lot recently because the words really resonated with my situation with the X Man and I used to sit there singing it feeling really sorry for myself. I used to say it was my anthem! It is called 'People Help the People'.

In one fell swoop two apparently disparate thoughts had neatly synchronised and the channel for my life purpose had been born.

## View from the Ground

The white feather? Was that a turning point? Definitely.

Viv and I love to walk and talk. We have both mentioned that we had immersed ourselves in a lot of negativity, but slowly we were rising out of that sad phase. As Viv has said, she was focussed – I might say, obsessed on seeing white feathers. My observations more often than not when we saw white feathers were 1) it was that time of year where birds drop feathers; 2) we have a lot of birds in the area we are lucky enough to live in; and 3) some poor bird has met its end thanks to the local cat.

However, that windy day – it was a Sunday – when the white feather danced in front of us – really changed my way of thinking. Maybe I could get on the journey, which has already being referred to.

I have already referred to the Law of Attraction and that really was the start of my process of seeing and understanding. More importantly, I could start to understand what Viv was experiencing and why she is keen to share it with as many people as possible. I even decided to try the idea of visualising something I would like to see – to put out there into the air / the universe what I wanted to see. I'm a sceptic, some would cruelly say cynic.

So, one morning, when I was travelling to another part of the country I visualised seeing a 'peacock' – it could be the word, a picture of the bird, whatever. I wasn't overly specific. To be fair, I put it out of my mind – until on my journey home, on a main commuter road I had to apply my brakes suddenly as there, crossing the road in front of me was, I know you know what I'm going to say ......................... a peacock.

I hope, by now, you are seeing how Viv's story really is one of an ordinary person experiencing extraordinary experiences which have helped shape the rest of her, and my, life.

**Jon**

# Synchronicity

*"I am open to the guidance of synchronicity and do not let expectations hinder my path"*
*DALAI LAMA*

This is worth a mention because it happens more and more in my life and in the lives of people around me.

Carl Jung came up with the theory of synchronicity and I think the best place to start is with a dictionary definition:

'The experience of two or more events that are apparently causally unrelated or unlikely to occur together by chance, yet are experienced together in a meaningful manner.'

I would agree with the Dalai Lama on this one. I very much see synchronicity as a 'sign' that you are on track with your life purpose. To me it is the Law of Attraction coming into play. Seemingly random things start happening to you which when pieced together create something rather exciting.

A lot of people would call this 'coincidence' and I have now learnt that there is no such thing as coincidences. If something happens that you think is a coincidence it is because your thoughts and the thoughts of someone else have manifested themselves in a synchronised way. It made me think of the term 'on the same wavelength'. I think this is another great example of a little phrase that we use a lot which has more meaning than we initially think. Thoughts will be synchronized if they are operating at the same energy frequency.

I think we have all experienced synchronicity to varying degrees in our lives. How many times has someone kept popping into your head? You might not have seen them for ages and then suddenly they call you or you bump into them at the shops.

How many times have you been singing a song and you turn the radio on and that very song is playing? You're usual reaction is "Oh, what a coincidence." or "Ha – I'm psychic". I now believe this is 'synchronicity' in action.

What I found amazing is that once I had got my head sorted out and understood where I was going and the skills I needed to get there, that suddenly everything started to fall into place. It almost felt like it was out there just waiting for me to realise the path I should be on and then it all started flying towards me.

I was reminded of this on a number of occasions when asking my angels for help (yes by now I had started communicating quite regularly!) where I was told very clearly to 'go with the flow' and 'get on the slip stream'.

Like the Dalai Lama, I now take anything that seems like a coincidence very seriously and acting on this intuition has stood me in good stead so far and brought some wonderful people into my life.

I am completely confident that the answers are there for me to give guidance on moving forward and I am open to how they come to me. Sometimes it will be a song that suddenly resonates with me or one that I hear over and over again. Sometimes I will just open the page of a book and read a paragraph that gives me the very answer to a question I have been mulling over.

Here's the very first, obvious realisation I had of synchronicity. I had been doing some work on establishing my life purpose and had been running through some of the questions I mentioned in Chapter 1. One of the things it had highlighted to me is that one of the happiest times of my career was when I used to mentor business start-ups in some quite deprived areas in Leeds. I loved hearing about their community based businesses and got a huge sense of fulfilment out of thinking I had influenced and inspired them to keep going and supported them (in a small way) in building their businesses. I also loved to hear about the businesses themselves. Most of them were social enterprises and were providing a service that directly supported their communities. There were some amazing stories of passion and belief that went into these businesses being started.

That night, I was thinking I would love to get involved in that type of work again because I hadn't done it for a while. The next morning I checked my inbox and there was an email from someone I didn't know and the subject heading was 'Splash'. I nearly didn't open it (I thought it was something to do with swimming!!) but a little voice in my head said "open it." As you know, I have previous experience of voices in my head so I do now listen to them seriously!

So I opened up the email and was covered from head to toe in goosebumps (or tingles as I now call them). By the way – tingles is another sign to show me I am right on track and doing what I should be doing. I get them all the time these days which shows that my life is getting more and more on track with my life purpose.

This email was from someone who had found me on Linked In (how many millions of people are there on Linked In?). They had looked at my profile and wondered if I would like to volunteer at a local College for a day. The event was to help young people develop their business ideas and for a group of experienced business people to mentor and coach them in developing their business idea and then play a bit of a 'Dragon's Den' at the end to see which group had the best idea.

I got that 'tingles' moment again. I didn't even have anything on my profile about mentoring businesses. How the heck did they find me? That's what you call synchronised. They needed volunteers to provide business mentoring to their students; I wanted to be a business mentoring volunteer. We were both on the same wavelength. It happened!

Another example of synchronicity involved my friend Jean (more about Jean later). One day out of the blue she said, "Has Ben had any thoughts or dreams recently?" Ben is my son and he had certainly not talked about any thoughts or dreams that had resonated with me but I resolved to log this in my memory bank has Jean's hunches are usually very accurate.

That evening I was having a general chit chat with Ben. We were talking about some motivational movies he had done and I had been asking him to do me one to help me with my new positivity resolve and visualising. I said he should do it as a business. He was looking at a picture of me in the dining room. (It's the photo of me on the back of this book.)

BEN: "When did you have that picture taken?"

ME: "When I won a Business Award."

BEN: "You ought to write a book you know."

I now believe that there is no such thing as a coincidence – it is synchronicity.

I use it as a gauge to show me what frequency I am operating at and some important guidance from a higher place that I am on the right path.

## The Flock Begins to Congregate

*"Friendship is born at that moment when one*
*man says to another: "What! You too?*
*I thought that no one but myself . . ."''*
CS LEWIS – THE FOUR LOVES

My life was beginning to improve dramatically. Not only was I feeling happier, healthier and more relaxed but I was very clear on the vision of my future and what would bring me fulfilment and happiness in my personal and work life.

I was back on track and very quickly some pretty wonderful people began to gather around me. Some new people, some people who had been associates in the past and we had kind of lost touch and other people who I was already close to and our relationship moved up another few levels.

The commonality was that they all shared the same values and beliefs as me; they were all on a journey of self-discovery and they all had very similar aspirations and desires in terms of their futures. The Law of Attraction and synchronicity were both beginning to work in my life.

I also began to see the contrast of Dark and Light between these people and others in my life. This helped my resolve to keep going through the turbulence that was now also starting to happen because people that no longer served my life purpose were beginning to 'de-manifest'.

Reflecting back over this lovely time of people gathering around me, I have also seen that each of them played their very important part in my life and development. I sincerely hope I have played an important part in their life story too.

It has honestly felt like they were sent to me for a reason and that reason was to keep me on track with my life purpose and to have the strength and courage to do it.

So here is a quick story on each and the amazing synchronicity that has happened with them being in my life.

## Jean

I knew Jean through my work. We were passing acquaintances who met occasionally within a group of other people in the equality and inclusion circles. The first time I properly spoke to Jean was at a meeting in London where we discovered that not only did we both live in Leeds - we actually lived just five minutes down the road from each other! There had been a time where Jean and I nearly worked on a project together – but the personalities around us put a stop to this and I now know this was for a reason.

We had lost touch for well over a year and then one day, shortly after I had my 'light bulb' moment about People Help People I got an email out of the blue from Jean, asking if I fancied meeting for a coffee. I was intrigued and we arranged a date.

We had a lovely catch up, mainly talking about what had been going on in our professional lives. Jean was at a cross roads and was feeling a little uncertain about her future. I was doing my best to stay positive about the X Man and the negativity around me. Despite not knowing Jean too well, we both naturally began to really open up to each other – it was just what we both needed.

We parted, vowing to stay in touch and not leave it so long next time and were just moving to our cars when Jean looked at me with knowing eyes and said, "You're quite spiritual aren't you." I was a little taken aback, mainly because I didn't think it was recognisable to others and also because I was quite surprised at how brave Jean was to ask that question. I am so glad she did because it was from that point onwards that we developed a truly deep and loving friendship.

Many of the tools and techniques I have learned and applied over the last few months have been given to me by Jean and she has truly given a massive turbo boost to my development. Jean has a gift of foresight and I know this is because she is very in touch with her intuition and higher guidance. It has helped guide her own life and now she was very kindly sharing that intuition with me. It was Jean that instigated my journey in writing this book. It was she who asked me if Ben (my son) had had any thoughts or dreams recently and that very evening he said I should write a book. Talk about synchronicity!

Although she constantly tells me off for 'putting her on a pedestal' (and I am sure she will have words to say when she reads this book!!!), what I have learned from Jean over the past few months has moved me to another level.

She has been the kind, thoughtful, yet firm word I needed when I was swaying in indecision and I feel calm and at peace in her company. Others say this about her too, so she is going to have to stop being so modest!

Jean's role in my life? - ENCOURAGING MY SPIRITUAL GROWTH. She is first and foremost a dear friend. She is also my spiritual mentor and guide and is now my business partner. Thanks Jean.

## Anj

Anj is an amazing lady. I have known Anj for many years and she has been a pretty constant throughout my time of running my own businesses. She has played quite a part directly and indirectly in me helping to develop my businesses and in a variety of roles. Firstly as my client; she has been a partner in a number of projects I have delivered and she has also worked very closely with me as an associate of my business. We were pretty much colleagues for well over a year and she therefore knows the X Man very well.

I have absolute respect for Anj as a business woman and she is highly regarded in professional circles. She is a lady who gets things done with a razor sharp focus and you can always rely on Anj to get results. She is also a fantastic relationship developer and her 'little black book' must be worth a fortune.

About a year ago, Anj lost a friend to suicide and it changed her view on the world. Within a month, I lost my dad and I think this developed even more of a bond between me and Anj, as we were grieving together.

It was shortly after this time that Anj made the decision to move on from our business. She had really tried to stay and support me but just could not tolerate the X Man's behaviour any longer, particularly in the light of her just losing her friend.

We have a rock solid relationship, so we continued to stay in touch and met relatively regularly for a chat over a glass of wine. I began to open up to Anj about some of the spiritual experiences I was having. To be honest, I wasn't really sure how Anj would react – she seems like such a 'grounded' person I thought she might think I had gone a bit bananas. So it was really reassuring to have such a positive reaction and to hear that she had also started on this spiritual path of discovery herself.

Our relationship stepped up another level and I began to get very strong intuitive feelings that Anj and I were going to be business partners.

Whenever I thought about Anj, I just thought 'energy' and 'vibrancy' and this was exactly what I needed in my life and to move my business idea forward as I was a little depleted on this front!

When I launched the Linked In group – it captured Anj's heart and we started to talk more and more about it but neither of us raised the point of us working together. Not sure why we were pussy footing around here. Perhaps it was just because neither of us really knew what the other was thinking and it was also very early days since my 'light bulb' moment.

Well, in steps Jean again with her intuition and this story is amazing. Jean had been in touch with me to say she had experienced a waking dream about me and I was a 'high priestess' (pretty cool eh!) with emerald green flowing robes. She thought that might have been one of my past lives.

Shortly after, I arranged for Jean to meet Anj and Amanda. I am not sure why but for some reason when I was thinking about us all meeting up – it was more our personalities (or 'souls') that I was visualising in the room. Jean and I were quite old and wise; Amanda was very pure and calm and Anj was an exuberant child who was busting at the seams to learn and crack on with things.

When we got together – Jean said she would do some Angel Card readings. Anj picked three cards and in one of the cards was a child with a high priestess in green behind her!

Mmmmm. I think I was getting a strong message here.

I said to Anj, "We need to get together," and she said, "Yes, we do." I think we both knew it was quite a momentous occasion (I seem to be having more and more of those these days!).

It was from our next meeting that our new business was born.

Anj's role in my life? – ENERGY & VITALITY!!!! She has bags of it in abundance and this is just what is needed in any business. She has always been a close friend and now she is also my business partner. Thanks Anj.

## Amanda

As you will recall, Amanda was one of the people on my list to tell them about my 'bath experience'.

Amanda is truly the most serene person I know. She has this glow about her and I feel her aura is so strong that even us mere mortals can see it. I often described Amanda as being 'like an angel' and so did others.

Amanda had already begun her spiritual journey and my story was like a gentle push for her to focus a bit more on it. She had been through a bit of a tough time in her life and had come out of it bravely and courageously. I saw her as a role model in terms of how to deal with the X Man and come out the other end smiling and more fulfilled as a person. Following my chat with her, we became 'travellers' together on this amazing journey.

This was great because Amanda was coming at things from a slightly different angle to me – so we often sat down together and compared notes on our new discoveries. She has also been a very willing guinea pig for some of the new techniques I have learned and has a great way of interpreting some of the things that have happened in my life recently.

Recently, Amanda has discovered a talent for painting which she didn't know she had and it seems to just flow so naturally out of her. I am honoured to now have an 'original' painting which Amanda did just for me at a time when I needed a lot of love and comfort. It is one of the most precious things I own.

Amanda's role in my life? – PURITY! She is also a very dear friend to me and we are very close business associates. Amanda has also been inspired to paint the picture for the cover of my book. It was channelled from a higher source and is awe inspiring. Thanks Amanda.

## Bernie

Bernie is a new person in my life. Synchronicity played a big part here. I had already been thinking I wanted to widen out the kind of support I gave to businesses and very much focus it around measuring social value that organisations delivered in their communities. This was exactly the field of work that Bernie had been in for many years.

Bernie joined the Linked In group I set up for People Help People and as we were both local we arranged to meet up. For various reasons we couldn't meet as arranged and - as often happens – other things took over and we never got that meeting.

However the Universe was not going to let us get away with this. We were clearly destined to work together and in stepped Jean, again!. She had also connected with Bernie via the Linked In group and they arranged to meet. Following that meeting, Jean said to me, "You must meet Bernie."

The rest, as they say, is history! Bernie is a lovely, kind, gentle person and one of those people that you just instantly get on with and feel like you have known them for ever. Her depth of business experience is exceptional.

Bernie's role in my life? – WARMTH, HUMOUR AND KNOWLEDGE. A lovely new friend who shares the same values and aims as me and the other people in my life. She is now also involved in our business! Thanks Bernie.

I was beginning to grow in confidence about telling my story. Not one person so far had pooh poohed it or disappeared out of my life - quite the opposite in fact. I found that most people were already on this journey. They were just keeping fairly quiet about it. However, everybody I had told so far was someone I already knew and to a certain extent could gauge very quickly if they were feeling uncomfortable with what I was saying.

Well the Universe wasn't going to let that carry on for too long. As much as I have a wonderfully large circle of family and friends, I would soon run out of people to tell and I don't think I would achieve my bigger life purpose if I just stuck to people I know. In steps Ryan the Window Cleaner!

## Ryan the Window Cleaner

I bet you didn't expect this as a heading in my book. Neither did I – but Ryan has played a fundamental role in my journey – even though he and I didn't initially realise it.

Ryan was a client of mine. He is a sole trading, window cleaner and I had helped him achieve an equality accreditation. I will always remember the first telephone conversation I had with Ryan because he's lovely and we had a bit of a laugh together. He was also very conscientious and sincere in achieving his accreditation and we had a lot of dialogue during this time as he wanted to make sure he was doing everything just right.

I spoke to him so often, I even programmed his name into my phone, so I could say "Hi Ryan." when he rang.

One day, shortly after he had achieved his accreditation, he rang to say he was going to a client meeting to tender for some work and could I pull out all the stops to get his certificate to him as he wanted to take it with him to the meeting. I made sure he got his certificate and asked him to let me know how he had got on.

That evening I got a call from him and it went something like this:

ME: "Hi Ryan. How did it go?"

RYAN: Sounding slightly distracted. "Oh yeah it went really well but I wanted to talk to you about something else."

ME: "Ooh that sounds intriguing. Tell me more."

RYAN: "I was in a refuge for women who had experienced domestic violence and there were a lot of teenage kids in there. I got talking to the kids and they were all saying how frustrating it was trying to get a job - bit of a Catch 22. They couldn't get a job because they had no work experience, but they couldn't get work experience because they couldn't get a job. I really felt for them as they all seemed quite low about it. I then walked into the office and the case workers were all really frustrated because of all the office work they had to do and they couldn't find the time to do it. It was like I had a light bulb moment. I said to them "Why don't you give the kids some work experience on a voluntary basis?" and it was like you could hear a pin drop in the room. They all stood there in stunned silence then said "What a fantastic idea". I don't know where this thought came from but it just popped into my head."

ME: "Wow – that is amazing. Why did you think to call me?"

RYAN: "I don't know. I just thought of you straight away and picked up my phone and your name was right in front of me. I just knew you would help me with this idea."

Well from that moment on, Ryan and I stayed in very regular contact and the idea just grew and grew between us.

His call had been so timely. I was realising that my original idea for a business wasn't quite so original and there was already a lot of great work going on regarding connecting business and community organisations.

I had also been getting a lot of 'messages' to 'slow it down' and was feeling that I needed to step back a bit and think about what service it was that People Help People was going to deliver. Ryan's call was timed to perfection (synchronicity again!) and helped me to move in the right direction.

In the weeks that followed, we spoke more and more and it was clear that Ryan was as committed and passionate about supporting people in communities as I was.

I also began to tentatively discuss some of the more 'spiritual' experiences I had been having and was delighted that Ryan didn't run a mile – in fact, quite the opposite – he positively embraced it all and recognised that something pretty special was happening. Jean also played a big part in this and looking back I realise she was gently nudging me to open up to Ryan and gave me the courage to do it. We ended up having some quite deep discussions about what was going on in our lives and realised there were a lot of parallels in terms of challenging people we both felt trapped by.

I must also add that at this point I had not met Ryan as he lives down South, but we had very rapidly developed a relationship of working together and I was getting the great opportunity to mentor and coach him in developing his business ideas (which was one of the things I had re-discovered I really enjoyed doing).

Ryan's role in my life journey? – MY OUTER WORLD TEST AND REFLECTION. I often used to say that Ryan was my 'prompt' and my 'conscience' and a reflection of my inner self in the outside world. If ever I was feeling a bit uncertain about how I was moving forward, you could guarantee Ryan would call and unbeknownst to him, get me right back on track in our discussion. Through our discussions, he has helped me see the bigger picture and the jigsaw pieces then started to fall neatly into place. He is probably the person that I have most felt the phenomena of 'synchronicity' with. I feel that his positive reaction to things is a reflection of how others will react and he has increased my confidence to talk openly to people that I didn't know without the fear of ridicule. He is now very much a part of our business and my life. Thanks Ryan.

I am hoping by now that I have given you a good understanding of the key things I have learned about the power of your mind and how this manifests itself in your life.

I also hope I have been able to pull all those jigsaw pieces together for you. I have discovered that I love connecting things. Whether that is people, companies or information – I get a real buzz out of connecting things to support better relationships, growth and understanding.

I have really enjoyed making all the connections between the scientific, religious, psychological and spiritual things I have learned about the immense power of our minds and sincerely hope I have made this knowledge accessible for you with my down-to-earth Yorkshire approach.

I also hope that you can see how you can play a very proactive part in developing your mind and I am going to focus on this in the remaining chapters of this book.

I will now be focussing on some of the key techniques I have learned that will help you to continue to grow and harness the power of your mind.

## View from the Ground

Three chapters don't even scratch at the surface of what has been a magnificent journey for Viv. Through her learning, it has inspired me and I am grateful to be able to add a few words to her story – but this really is just a start.

This really is a story of moving from dark to light; from negative to positive; from despair to hope and belief.

It's a lesson on never allowing anyone to control your life and make you feel lacking in value. No one has that right. But in reality, it only happens if you allow it to.

Easier said than done, but I truly hope you find Viv's story the inspiration that fires you to take whatever action you need to take and maintain control of your own life.

It really is about focusing on what you have and what you want, not what you haven't and what you are jealous about someone else having. It is about focussing on what you can give, because if you give you get back in abundance. A daft example here is at our local Indian take away (please note, no product placement in this book). I am the hunter gatherer in our house – in other words, I collect the take away every week. I always make sure I am happy (even when the food's not ready) and have a pleasant chat to the staff at the take away. Through developing that relationship, more often than not, we find surprise 'compliments of the chef' extras in our food bag, and other freebies. I remember one time the freebies were 25% of the value of the order.

A small example, maybe, but it works for me.

Enjoy reading on.

**Jon**

# CHAPTER 4

## The Exhilaration of Flying

*"When I was 5 years old my mother always told
me that happiness was the key to life.
When I went to school, they asked me what
I wanted to be when I grew up.
I wrote down 'happy'.
They told me I didn't understand the assignment,
and I told them they didn't understand life."*
*JOHN LENNON*

A few years ago I bought Jon a book for his birthday called "I Can Make you Happy" by hypnotherapist Paul McKenna.

It was actually a bit of a joke because Jon is (or should I say 'was') well known for being a little on the pessimistic side. At the same time I also bought him one called "I Can Make You Slim" – it's no wonder he is paranoid about his weight, poor man!!

Little did I know that in a year's time, this book would be my first 'life saver' as I was dealing with the worst of the challenges I was going through.

I would also say there was a massive amount of synchronicity going on here. The book had been lost in the depths of our bookshelves and had never been read (sorry Paul!). Jon clearly thought he was happy enough and didn't need any help. Then one weekend when I had just about hit rock bottom, I was doing my usual Saturday morning chore of cleaning. I don't know why but for some reason I had an urge to polish the bookshelves (I never get that urge.....ever!). As I dusted away I knocked a book off the shelf and there it was. It literally felt like it had been put there rather precariously for me to knock off the shelf. I asked Jon if he had moved it to the front of the shelves and he gave me the raised eyebrow look as if to say "Do you really think I would be reading that?" (sorry again Paul!).

I took it as a sign, given I definitely needed something to make me happy at that particular moment in time – so I began to read.

This was the first book I had actually read that focussed on the 'mind' and how to master it. Up to that point I had just been reading fairly spiritual things about earth angels and the Universe etc and it was really Paul's book that gave me a more 'scientific' angle, but the amazing thing was I could see complete cross over with some of the stuff I had been reading about angels and the spirit world.

On reading the book I had a massive realisation that this is an 'inside job' and I'm not talking about a big bank raid! We have so much power in our mind that we really can overcome anything if we put our mind to it. I realised that it really didn't matter that I was still facing all the challenges that were currently in my life, the important thing was how I chose to deal with them.

I realised that it was no use trying to control every situation in my life and the outer environment I was already in. I certainly realised that it was absolutely no use trying to control the X Man – he was the master of controlling so it was just useless trying to compete. This was what had got me into this downward spiral in the first place because I had focussed all my energy on 'counter-controlling' tactics and not on the most important thing – the damage this was doing to me 'inside'.

I was on a very slippery slope of negative thoughts and emotions and the more I thought about my outward environment, the worse it got. Well of course it did! I was focussing on something almost 24/7 (I wasn't sleeping very well at the time!) so was giving it real power to manifest and was then charging it with negative emotions.

A key to raising your 'energy' field and therefore attracting positive things into your life is to be happy. It's as simple as that.

Now, I was in a pretty dark place and the last thing I was feeling was happy, so I had to find some pretty neat tricks to get myself into a happy state and Paul McKenna's book set me on that path.

I discovered that our happiness is founded in our personal values. I had already worked out that my external environment at work was not letting me live these values and I was beginning to make changes in this respect. Values are what give meaning to your life and help guide you to your life purpose so I was pretty clear on this front. However, this seemed like a longer term goal (a bit like turning a big ship around in the ocean) as I had a lot of things to sort out. I really NEEDED instant gratification in terms of lifting my spirits (ha just realised that is a phrase we use regularly without really thinking of its deeper meaning!)

What I really needed were some techniques that could help give me a bit of a 'lift' despite everything that was going on around me and it was from this point on that I discovered some very simple, yet amazingly effective techniques to raise my happiness levels.

## Happiness and Discovering Your Inner Child

*"..Dance like there's nobody watching you*
*Love like you'll never be hurt*
*Sing like there's nobody listening*
*And live like it's heaven on earth"*
*WILLIAM W PURKEY*

By now I had realised that happiness comes from within.

No one else can make you happy. Happiness is a state of your own mind and sometimes when you are in a difficult environment and have a lot of worries and concerns it does seem almost impossible to be happy.

I often used to think, "How the heck can I be happy with all this negative stuff going on in my life!"

What I found was that there were some things I could do really quickly which would begin to lift my spirits and act as a foundation for everything else I was doing to re-discover my natural state of positivity and optimism.

I acknowledged that it would be unrealistic to expect to be deliriously happy every second of the day when there were negative things going on around me. However, I knew that if I could come at things from a slightly happier and more positive angle it would have huge benefits in helping me to cope with the pressures I was facing.

If you are like me, you will probably have experienced that 'sinking feeling' countless times. This is a physical manifestation of your unhappiness. I used to get this feeling all the time and there were a lot of occasions where I just felt permanently 'low'. This wasn't just because of what was going on in my mind and outer environment. It was actually the physical effect it was having on my body.

There are a number of chemicals that are produced in your body when you are in a stressful situation and these are fine if you are just about to run away from a man-eating tiger or fight a dinosaur. I was not doing either of these things. I was sitting at my desk trying to figure out how to deal with life! Unfortunately these chemicals can do serious damage if left to fester, so I discovered that to relieve these physical concerns I almost had to replicate the physical activity that the chemicals were getting me ready to embark on i.e. get up from behind my desk and do some energetic activity. For me this meant walking or dancing. Mainly walking and I became known as the Forrest Gump of the family.

There are also other things you can do physically which give you an instant pick me up and make you feel a little stronger than perhaps you were previously.

The first one I tried was imagining you have a hook at the top of your head with a gold thread tied to it. Imagine that this gold thread is tugging gently on the hook pulling you upwards. Try it – it seriously works. I've never been a 'stooper' but this is something it is so easy to do if you are feeling a bit down in the dumps. I used to imagine this hook and gold thread whenever I went out for a walk. I found it instantly put a spring in my step because I was feeling like something was pulling me upwards with every step.

I combined this with making sure I was looking upwards as often as possible. Now you do have to be a bit careful with this one if you are out walking. Firstly because you might step in something unsavoury on the ground that you had not seen because you were looking upwards and secondly you might crash into someone if you are looking heavenwards and not focussing on where you are going!

Seriously though – this really does work. It is natural to look downwards more when we are feeling a bit down. Looking upwards really does give you an instant pick me up.

Smiling and laughing are great pick me ups for making you feel happy. It is impossible to smile and not feel better. Laughing brings the added benefit of a physical release aswell, which is great to get rid of those unwanted chemicals. I purposefully stopped watching anything miserable on TV (including the news). If the news came on the radio, I would switch it off. I know this might sound a bit selfish in a way but I realised that listening to more bad news in other people's lives just wasn't helping me. It was programming even more negativity into my mind. I made sure that everything I watched on TV was positive and if it was humorous and I could have a good old belly laugh then that was even better.

Music and dancing have always been my saviours. I have always loved dancing with complete abandon at family parties, much to Jon's embarrassment (he has been known to call me 'Skippy' on the dance floor!). Dancing is such a fantastic release and if you can do it 'like nobody is watching' then even better because it gives you a huge positive workout.

I would also combine it with 'singing like nobody is listening' for a turbo boost of positivity. This really did give me an instant pick me up and drive everyone else out of the room!

Jon has made me a number of playlists on his IPod which I play on a regular basis when I am at home and dance around the dining room with as much vigour as I can. I do think the next door neighbours are getting slightly concerned now at this mad woman careering past the window every now and then waving her arms around. You see – even when I know people are watching me I dance as if they aren't!

Live music is even better. You have a license to jump up and down waving your arms wildly, whilst screaming when you are at a concert. That is the norm…isn't it? Again, I do seem to have a knack of embarrassing my family at concerts. There is usually a bit of a battle as to who is going to sit next to me (the further away the better for my lovely husband and children!). Joking apart though – my enthusiasm usually rubs off pretty quickly on the rest of the family and they also abandon their inhibitions.

Another technique is to place a number of 'cues' around your house that act as little prompts for you to have a positive thought. Paul McKenna suggests dots or post it notes. As you move around your house and see these dots it prompts you to think of a positive memory and something that made you feel happy. It also creates quite an interesting talking point when people visit your house!

Have you ever watched young children play? They are usually laughing and skipping around and completely living in the moment.

I wasn't living in the moment at all – I was mulling over the past way too much and worrying about the future in equal measure. I realised I was wasting my life away and I really did need to start living in the moment and opening my eyes to everything wonderful around me.

Young children have no inhibitions. They are not weighted down with the worries of the world on their shoulders and they love every minute of their lives (well apart from when they don't get that toy or chocolate bar they wanted!). They view the world almost with awe. I remember going out for a walk one day and there was a mum and her young children ahead of me. It was spring and one of the children ran over to a tree and his little face lit up. He shouted "Wow – look at these flowers – they look like yellow church bells!" His mum did have to make a swift intervention to stop him picking all those daffodils from under the tree but it was like another light bulb moment for me. I had walked past those daffodils so many times and not even noticed them. In an instant I saw them through the eyes of that child and they took on a whole different perspective. I resolved to try and rediscover my inner child.

Now when I am out on my walks it is like a whole new world has opened up and I am viewing everything with a fresh pair of eyes. You cannot help but be happy when you are living in the moment out in nature – it is truly awesome! Focussing on seeing everything around me whilst out walking is almost meditative and I find it incredibly uplifting.

I began to think back to my childhood and some of the things I really enjoyed doing.

*Walking through piles of leaves and kicking them all up in the air (sorry Jon – more embarrassment when you have been out on walks with me!!)
*Blowing dandelion seeds
*Making daisy chains
*Colouring in
*Getting to the top of a hill on my bike. Setting off and kicking my legs in the air and shouting "Wheeeeeeeeeeeeeeeeee!"
*Splashing in the sea and being bowled over by massive breakers
*Making sandcastles
*Dressing up
*Playing make believe
*Having an imaginary friend
*Being a super hero
*Cutting out, gluing and sticking
*Trampolining (sorry – more embarrassment for my family although it is well hidden at the bottom of the garden. Hope the neighbours can't hear my 'whooping')
*Fun fair rides – you can't beat a good old scream with a reasonable excuse to do so

It's almost like I was creating a new version of a bucket list. To heck with visiting the Seven Wonders of the World. I want to do some colouring in!

Jean and I recently ran a workshop for people who wanted to try and connect with their angels. What a wonderful experience and honour to lead them through this process (and certainly something I would never have anticipated doing a couple of years ago!). In the last session we got out a big box of chubby crayons and some colouring pencils and gave everyone a Mandala to colour in. I have never seen a room full of adults slip so quickly into complete and utter concentration and enjoyment. It was a wonderful sight to watch and one that reaffirmed to me just how important it is to not forget your inner child.

Playing 'make believe' is also a great one. Day-dreaming has got itself a bad name. I think sitting quietly and imagining your perfect life is a great way to boost the spirits. There is a whole industry that has set up around this – to help people 'visualise' their dreams and manifest them into reality. I find this kind of activity an instant pick me up. Just sitting quietly and imagining what would be my perfect life and trying to get it as detailed as possible. This can be done on a deeper level in meditations and hypnosis but just thinking about what you would like, and imagining that you have it does make you feel happy.

I also released my inner child and did a 'vision' board. I absolutely loved cutting out, gluing and sticking. It was really therapeutic.

Paul McKenna suggests 'The Happy Step In'. Here you think about someone you know or admire who is very happy. You try to imagine as vividly as possible everything about them. What they are wearing, how they are standing and what they are doing. You then walk up behind them and step into the person so you can see the world through their eyes and physically copy their posture and experience all their feelings. You notice where the feelings are strongest in your body and try to spread these feelings all over your body. You then imagine taking this feeling into your everyday life.

Having an 'imaginary friend' is a good one. I think the 'friend' is not imaginary at all and is quite possibly an angel or spirit guide that children just happen to be able to see because they don't have the filters us adults do. However my current 'imaginary friend' (apart from my guardian angel of course) is an alter ego superhero that actually came to me in a Shamanic Meditation (more about these later). She is a Red Indian Warrior and she is me in another lifetime. I often visualise her when I am having a difficult time and become her. She can usually be seen performing a great act of bravery and then standing very confidently and upright, hands on hips looking very proud about her act of courage. I know it sounds a bit daft but it really does help. If kids can be super heroes – why can't we?

Another technique I learned was to have some 'mood shifters' up your sleeve that you can call on in any given moment when needed. It feels to me a bit like the 5th emergency service and I have called on these many times over the last couple of years.

It is basically a number of memories of funny things that have really made you laugh or feel happy. I wrote these down and the process in itself was a positive one which made me laugh and smile while I was doing it. I just went for five memories to start with and I tried to jot them down in as much detail as possible so that I could really imagine them when I needed them. Even better, if it is people that you love it will give you an even warmer feeling when you remember them. I found that I came up with quite a few memories of the kids when they were younger and some of the funny things they did. When I am in a situation where I feel like I need a 'mood shifter' I imagine myself talking to the person involved in my memory and saying "Ha...do you remember when........" It instantly makes me feel better and evokes all those lovely memories of happy times, fun and laughter.

Another great way to give yourself instant happiness is to think about all the great things you have in your life and that you have received throughout your life and to be truly grateful for them.

# Count Your Blessings

*"Keep your eyes open to your mercies. The man who forgets
to be thankful has fallen asleep in life."*
ROBERT LOUIS STEVENSON

*"We learned about gratitude and humility – that so many people
had a hand in our success, from the teachers who inspired us to
the janitors who kept our school clean…and we were taught to
value everyone's contribution and treat everyone with respect."*
MICHELLE OBAMA

When I was a little girl, it was instilled in me to say thank you
for things and to be truly grateful. I was never keen on the
job of writing thank you letters to relatives after Christmas
and my birthday. It almost took away from the joy of getting
a present and felt quite dutiful. To all my relatives out there,
I hope you can forgive this admission. I realise now I was
pretty shallow (well what do you expect from a child/
teenager?). I was only young and didn't realise the true
value of gratitude.

If I was writing those letters now I would write so much
more.

I wouldn't just write 'thankyou for the present/money'.
I would write about the joy I got from the present. How
I played with it. How I used it. If I had received money I would
send a story of how I went shopping to spend the money and
what I bought and how it had enhanced my life (no matter
how small the way). I would try and send a photo of me with
the gift –so the kind person giving it to me could really feel
the happiness it had brought me.

Even though the letter would still be relatively 'dutiful' to the relative who had sent me the present/money – I would be thinking about how the letter might lift their spirits (there I go saying this phrase again!) but I would also gain a lot of pleasure in re-living a lovely time or imagining a lovely time ahead with my gift.

Transport me forward thirty odd years (or nearer forty if I was being completely honest!!)and I realised that I was so focussed on all the negative things in my life, that I had actually forgotten about all the good things in my life and was seriously taking them for granted. I was completely blinkered on the negative and was not seeing all the wonderful things in my life that I was truly blessed to have.

I read the most amazing book called "The Magic", by Rhonda Byrne and it quite literally turned my life around. The book was a continuance of the Law of Attraction theories and raising our 'vibrations' by being positive and 'giving' thanks, with the theory being that what you give out is what you get back. So if you are 'giving' thanks for things – you will get more of the same back.

I was definitely not counting my blessings – quite the opposite. I was focussing all my energies on what I didn't have. Was it any wonder that I was attracting this negativity into my life!!

Gratitude features significantly in a lot of religious scriptures.

"Whoever has will be given more, and he will have an abundance. Whoever does not have, even what he has will be taken from him" Gospel of Matthew

On the face of it, this doesn't actually sound very fair but if you consider that this passage is referring to 'gratitude' and not 'possessions' it takes on a whole new meaning

"Whoever has GRATITUDE will be given more, and he will have an abundance. Whoever does not have GRATITUDE, even what he has will be taken from him"

This was quite a profound moment for me. I thought back to some of the things I had lost or didn't have an abundance of (mainly money!) and realised I had been taking it all for granted.

The Koran follows the same approach:

"And Remember when God proclaimed: If you are grateful, I will give you more; but if you are ungrateful verily my punishment is indeed severe"

This was a massive turning point for me and probably another 'light bulb' moment because I realised that something as simple as gratitude was going to create some fundamental shifts in my life. Not only was it going to make me feel happier – it was also going to help me harness the Universal Laws (that are described in Holy Scriptures) to attract more 'blessings' into my life.

I quickly realised that 'gratitude' had to become a part of my life and I needed to commit myself to some conscious action in this respect.

The first thing I did was get myself a really nice notebook and I committed myself to getting up half an hour earlier every day to complete the 10 things I was most grateful for. Initially this was quite a challenge because I had been focussing on quite the opposite – all the things I really didn't want in my life and all my problems.

I found that once I got in the flow, I was astonished by just how much I did have to be grateful for and I began to get a whole new perspective on my life. Not only was I realising just how blessed I was, but thinking about all the good things in my life was having a fundamental effect on my mindset. It was almost like I was 'awakened' and my eyes were opened to all the wondrous things I had in my life. I actually felt (and still do) very humbled by this experience because I realised quickly just how truly blessed my life was.

Because it was initially a bit of a struggle to get started, I thought I would give you some extracts from my gratitude book to hopefully get your thinking on track and give you a few ideas for inspiration.

In addition to writing down 'what' I was grateful for, I found it really powerful to also add in 'why' I was grateful for things. It expanded my thinking out to the positive impact these 'blessings' had for me personally and shifted my mindset from the negative to the positive very quickly. Also, in writing these things down it slowed me down enough to really think about what I was grateful for and give it the full appreciation it deserved.

## Health and body

I am truly grateful for my health and my ability to walk because walking is one of the things I most love and it makes me feel energised and calm

I am truly blessed to have perfect hearing as I can hear all my loved ones' voices and I love listening to music as it brings me peace and joy

With all my heart – thank you for my good night's sleep because I feel energized (this was when Jon was going through a bit of a snoring phase!)

I am truly blessed to have healthy hands, fingers and arms because I could do some gardening yesterday which I absolutely love

I am truly blessed to have a healthy sense of smell because I can smell the fresh cut grass, lovely flowers, the soil and wonderful food cooking

I am truly blessed to have healthy eyes so I can see all the beauty around me

I am truly grateful that I can write, because this process every morning reminds me of just how much I do have to be grateful for

I am truly blessed to have a strong and healthy heart because it pumps life blood around my body and keeps all my other organs functioning

I am truly grateful for my flexible, supple neck and shoulders

## Work

I am so grateful to have some wonderful clients who have stayed loyal to us during difficult times in the business

I am blessed to have been asked to be a Trustee of Disability Sport Yorkshire because it has guided me to the path I am now on

I am so grateful to be able to work from home because I get to look out onto my beautiful garden when I am working

I am truly grateful that I run my own business because it is great being my own boss and it is exciting and challenging, bringing me new experiences every day

I am truly grateful for the deal I closed yesterday because it made me realise how good I am at developing relationships

I am truly grateful I met some important deadlines yesterday because it has enhanced my client relationship

I am so grateful I get to travel around and meet really interesting people

I am so grateful I have the confidence to present at events because it enables me to raise the profile of my business in a really positive way

I am really grateful for the comments I have received so far about People Help People because it makes me realise how needed this service is and how successful my future is going to be

## Money

I am so grateful for the money that our clients paid recently because it meant I could draw some money from the business and pay for things my family needs

I am truly grateful for our mortgage provider because they enable us to live in our wonderful house

To mum and dad. Thank you for all the money you paid throughout my life that enabled me to have food and drink; all the stuff I needed for school; my clothes and shoes; my bike and Action Girl; my music lessons; trips to the cinema; holidays and everything I needed for my daily needs (shampoo, toothpaste)

I am so grateful for all the money I have received in my life because it has bought many lovely things and enabled many special memories

I am truly grateful I was able to pay my credit card bills because I know I am reducing my debt and getting things in control

I am truly grateful that we have enough money to go to the pub for a glass of wine because it is so lovely sitting out in the sunshine, chatting to Jon about our days

I am truly grateful to mum for treating us to lunch for Ben's birthday and the weather was so wonderful. It was a perfect lunchtime.

## Possessions

I am truly grateful and blessed to live in such a beautiful house because it has a feeling of peace and happiness that everyone notices and it is our safe haven

I am truly grateful for my lovely car and the ability to drive as it enables me to travel far afield and meet interesting people in our business

I am so grateful for my beautiful garden because it is huge and full of lovely trees and flowers and it brings me peace and harmony when I am in it

I am so grateful for our television because I watched some great TV last night that made me laugh and moved me

I am truly grateful for my iron as it helps me make Jon's shirts look smart

I am truly grateful for my washing machine and my vacuum cleaner and all other household appliances as they all make life so easy

I am truly grateful for our radiators because it felt a bit chilly this morning and they warmed the house nice and quickly

I am truly grateful that we could buy Ben so many nice presents for his birthday because he really deserves them and is very happy with them

## Relationships

I am truly blessed to have Jon as my husband because he is my soul mate and my rock and he makes me feel safe, loved and happy

I am truly blessed to have Ben as my son because he is funny, caring and charming and he makes me laugh

I am truly blessed to have Livia as my daughter because she is thoughtful, unique and deep and she makes me feel peaceful and gives great cuddles

I am truly blessed and grateful to have my mum because she is so kind and loving and makes me feel safe and loved which gives me strength when I need it

With all my heart, thank you for bringing Jean back into my life because her words helped me to realise how much people think about me and it helped to re-build my self-esteem

I am so grateful to Jon for being a good listener because he helps me put a perspective on things and know that it is all going to come good

I am so grateful for the wonderful hugs I had from Ben and Livia yesterday as it made me feel so loved, peaceful, happy and calm

I am truly grateful that mum lives so nearby because it means I can see her quickly and regularly

I am blessed to have such a wonderful mum because I can talk to her openly about my spiritual journey and she understands and is fascinated

I am truly blessed to have a friend like Kathy in my life because she has helped me understand mindfulness and my true path

## Life

I am truly grateful and blessed to be alive!!!!

I am truly grateful to have discovered the power of my mind and ways I can harness it positively

I am truly blessed to live where I do in the beautiful countryside in an abundance of nature

I am truly blessed to be developing an understanding of the Universe and the power within me as it is enabling me to live my dreams

I am really happy and grateful to have our Saturday lunch routine because what better thing is there in life than sitting round a table with your loved ones eating fine food and drinking fine wine

I am truly blessed to be surrounded by wonderful people in my life because they all make me feel loved, respected, happy and protected

I am so grateful to Kathy for helping me to get on the right path because I know I am heading in the right direction for my life purpose

I am truly grateful that I am now naturally having happy and grateful thoughts because it is shifting my life around and helping me see the abundance I already have in my life

I am truly happy and grateful that Kathy helped me discover the power of meditation. I really enjoyed my first class today and found it really calming

## Nature

I am so happy and grateful for the beautiful sunshine yesterday as it warmed my heart and made me feel blissful when I felt its warmth on my face.

I am truly grateful that we live so close to the Yorkshire Dales and the glory of nature is on my doorstep

I am truly grateful to the people we met yesterday on our walk in the Dales or we would have ended up completely lost!!!

However, I am also truly grateful that we did veer off track because it meant we saw some fantastic views of the 3 Peaks that we would not have otherwise seen

I am so grateful to have healthy eyes because I could gaze at the wonderful cherry blossom outside my bedroom window this morning.

I am truly grateful for the magical air I breathe as it is keeping me alive!!!

## Goods and Services

With all my heart, I thank you for the fresh, clean water that comes into my house every day because it is 'on tap' (literally!) whenever I need it

I am truly grateful for the wonderful fresh coffee I have every morning and to all the people involved in bringing that to me. The people who planted the coffee bean plants; the people who picked the coffee beans; the people who processed and packaged the coffee beans; the people who transported the coffee beans to the supermarket and of course my milkman who delivers milk to my doorstep.

I am truly grateful for the wonderful hot water I have instantly in my house that enables me to have relaxing baths and invigorating showers

I am truly grateful for all the wonderful services available to us in our house. To the dustbin men who collect our rubbish every week. To the police and fire service who protect us. To the gas and electricity providers that ensure we have unlimited gas and electricity whenever we need it

I am truly grateful for the NHS as this is a magnificent service for everyone in the UK and ensures my family and loved ones will always have medical care, free of charge, when needed

I hope this insight into my gratitude journal has given you a few pointers to get started on this path.

I still can't quite believe that I am grateful for my iron!!!! But do you know what. A chore that was something I hated has now honestly become a pleasure because the 'gratitude' process helped me to look at everything from a much wider and more appreciative perspective. OK – I'm not keen on ironing but I am blessed enough to have a wonderful husband and two wonderful kids that I can iron for. So I found myself thinking about Jon, Ben and Livia when I was ironing and it always made me feel happy.

I also get to choose what I watch on TV while I am ironing and no one can argue (that is a family rule!) so I have two things to be grateful for when I am doing the ironing because it is a rare moment indeed when I actually get the Sky remote control in my hand.

Same goes for cleaning. I have never enjoyed that chore and usually spent my time cleaning, thinking jealous thoughts about all those people who could afford cleaners. I was missing a trick!!! Firstly I am lucky enough to own a vacuum cleaner that makes the job so much easier. Secondly, I have a wonderful house with loads of wonderful things in it and cleaning gave me the chance to really see and appreciate what a wonderful house I live in. Again, I started to see everything with a whole new perspective and noticing just how much abundance I already had in my life - and not just abundance of money. This was making me realise how blessed I was to have many other things in my life that were far more important and precious than money and that I was 'wealthy' in love and relationships.

It has actually been a really lovely exercise looking back through my Gratitude Journal because it made me realise just what an amazing impact that being grateful started to have on my life. It is almost a representation of my journey as I discovered more and more to be grateful for. Things I would never have considered being grateful for and just took for granted.

It also shows that about halfway through (so after about fourteen days), magical things started to happen and it takes me back to this time of my life when I was really focussed on being grateful.

It was almost like magic or a miracle!! There were a number of shifts that started to unfold and make a marked improvement on my life.

Focussing on what I was grateful for and giving thanks for key things in my life began to have the positive Law of Attraction effect.

My relationship with friends and family, which was already good, began to take on a whole new dimension as I appreciated everything special and unique about each person in my life. Whereas before I had been stuck in my own little world of self-pity and become pretty grumpy as a result, I noticed that my newfound happiness was having a positive knock on effect with everyone around me.

My health improved dramatically as I was focussing on all the things I was grateful for about my health. There were some quite miraculous things. One really noticeable thing was that my eyesight became much stronger. I wore glasses just for watching TV at night when my eyes were a bit tired and for driving and I suddenly realised I hadn't worn my glasses for some time as I really didn't think I needed them. I thought perhaps this might be down to me actually properly 'seeing' the beautiful world around me so colours seemed to intensify, but then I went to have my regular eye test and was told I had near perfect 20-20 vision and I no longer needed to wear glasses. Wow – how amazing is that!

I had also stopped moaning about my sore neck and shoulders and had switched to expressing gratitude for my flexible, supple, relaxed neck and shoulders. Overnight the pain disappeared. It really did feel like a miracle.

I expressed gratitude for my strong, healthy immune system and I have not had one bug for over two years. If I feel a sniffle coming on, or I have been around people who have a cold or some illness, I focus on expressing gratitude for my healthy immune system and nothing takes a hold. It is quite amazing!

Focussing gratitude for my strong healthy heart brought down my heart rate and my blood pressure. This stuff really is magical.

At the time, because of all the negativity that had built up between me and the X Man, I was still pretty uncomfortable and unhappy in my job. However, I set myself the challenge of finding reasons why I was grateful for my job and here's what I came up with:

It gives me freedom to choose what I do

I can work from home and don't have a horrible commute stuck in traffic every day

I see my lovely garden every day

I get to travel and meet interesting people

The X Man – on a good day – is a mentally stimulating business partner

I have a great laptop and all the equipment I need

I plan my own day

I get to go out for a walk during the day

People respect me

People enjoy working with me

It has bought me some good income

I get to see Ben and Livia when they get home from school/University

I love having the freedom to develop new things and implement them quickly

We have some really great clients

I feel like I am having a direct impact on progressing the equality agenda in the UK

The X Man is a pretty driven individual and when he is in a good mood that motivates me

At work, I found that clients were coming back to me who had originally said they didn't want to use our services. Communicating with them suddenly seemed so easy and not the hard sales slog I had been feeling previously. The money started to come back into the business and it all just felt so positive and easy. Every client I spoke to was just so lovely and keen to go ahead working with us.

At the time, my relationship with the X Man even improved. This was because I set myself the challenge of finding 10 things about him that I was truly grateful for. I really thought this was going to be virtually impossible but it actually made me look at him in a whole new light and to see there was some good in there. I think this is a really useful exercise for anybody who is in a difficult relationship. It helped me to look at the different sides of the X Man that I had forgotten because I was weighed down with a bucket load of negative thoughts about him. It is actually quite a cathartic exercise to really set yourself the challenge of finding 10 things you are grateful for in someone or something that you feel is making your life a misery but it really did work. I admit I did find it difficult but actually delving into this made me realise how far I had come in a short space of time.

Here's what I managed to come up with and I hope this helps you if you are in a difficult relationship right now:

I am grateful for your business mind because I have learned so much from you

I am grateful for your wicked sense of humour because when you are in good spirits you really make me laugh

I am grateful for your technology skills because they have enabled us to move our business into a new innovative direction

I am grateful that it has been tough working with you because it has strengthened me as an individual and made me realise I can deal with anything. What doesn't kill you makes you stronger!

I am grateful for your criticism and challenges because it has made me realise that I am actually a strong person and this is helping me to rebuild my self-esteem

I am grateful for you being the most challenging person I have ever worked with because it has jolted me to review my values; re-set my path and get on track with my life purpose

I am grateful for your kind hospitality when me and my family have visited you

I am grateful that you have taught me a lot about how to be very careful when making decisions about who I work with

I am grateful that I have now learned to follow my 'gut instinct' and intuition and to be led by my heart and not my head

I am grateful that your behaviour has pushed me to take a really good look inside at myself and I am the happiest and most content I have been for many years

Another technique I learned – which links in with the Law of Attraction was to start being grateful for things I wanted in my life. I found this a great way to start 'dreaming' that I already had the things I wanted.

This technique was one of the first and most profound that I used. It very quickly moved from me being grateful consciously to me being grateful subconsciously and I now find that I just automatically think for the things I am grateful for in any situation whether good or bad. I am a right 'Pollyanna' these days, but joking apart it is such a simple approach and yet raises the positivity bar massively.

My central heating boiler broke recently. A couple of years ago I would have thought the world was against me and yet my immediate (almost!) mindset when I was told I would need a new boiler was to think of all the positives and what I was grateful for in this situation.

It really is a much better way to approach life.

THANKYOU THANKYOU THANKYOU!

## Love

*"All good feelings come from love!*
*All negative feelings come from lack of love."*
RHONDA BYRNE

*"The Power of Love – a force from above*
*Cleaning my soul…"*
FRANKIE GOES TO HOLLYWOOD – THE POWER OF LOVE

If you are anything like me, when someone says the word love to you it immediately conjures up images of loved ones and how you feel about them.

I have learnt that there is so much more to the word 'love'.

Love is energy and is actually the highest frequency energy that any of us can feel and give out.

I have discovered that powering things with love really did 'clean my soul' and that it is a major force in the Law of Attraction.

I began to think about all the wonderful things in my life that I loved and I could see why I had attracted them to me – because the energy I was giving off when thinking about any of them was the most powerful frequency I could be giving off.

I hadn't really thought about it so deeply before but I realised that the things that make me happy are things I love; the things that make me grateful are things I love; the things that help me stay positive are all things I love and the special people in my life are all people I love.

Love is also a massive motivator. I work extra hard towards achieving anything that I know I am going to love.

Conversely I do not give much energy at all to things I don't love and this was quite an enlightening thought for me.

It made me realise that the areas in my life where I was not doing as well as I wanted to must have something in there that I didn't love. As a result I was avoiding them or procrastinating in terms of doing something because it just wasn't lighting my fire.

I also realised that I had a word in my vocabulary that was doing me a lot of damage and that word was the polar opposite of 'love'. I may not have used the word 'hate' towards any particular person (although I might have been nearly driven to it with the X Man on a number of occasions!) but I realised that I did have that word in my vocabulary for a lot of the situations I was in.

Having a greater understanding of how the conscious and subconscious minds work led me to the worrying conclusion that I had been programming a lot of hate into my mind and that as the subconscious mind doesn't distinguish between what is real and what is imaginary, I was unwittingly creating a load of situations in my mind that were being created into my reality.

I certainly didn't want any more situations in my life that I hated so I resolved to remove the word from my vocabulary. It even feels a bit weird typing it now because I cannot imagine ever feeling such a strong and negative emotion about anything ever again.

It feels absolutely wonderful to think about things you love. I usually get that excited feeling and it gives me tingles. I can almost feel the positive energy rising up a frequency and bursting out of me.

I resolved to introduce a bit of time in my day to think about the things I loved and to recognise things I loved in my day-to-day routine while going about my business.

Much the same as gratitude, I realised that there were so many things in my life that I loved and that these were the things I needed to focus on to keep my energy vibrations up!

Because my outer environment was pretty tough and stressful, I must admit it was initially a bit of a challenge to come up with a huge list that didn't just include my friends and family. So I thought it might be helpful if I gave you some extracts from my 'Love List' to hopefully get you started:

I Love Jon's twinkly eye's when he smiles (sorry to embarrass you Jon!)

I Love my trips to the pub with Jon

I Love Ben's gorgeous face (I'm a bit biased as he is my son!)

I Love the chats I have with Ben when we are out for walks

I Love Liv's lovely cuddles

I Love Liv's sense of justice

I Love mum's sparkly smile

I Love the sanctuary of mum's house

I Love Kathy's goodness and kindness

I Love Kathy's maverickness (I don't think that is a proper word but hopefully you understand my meaning)

I Love Leeds!!

I Love Barcelona

I Love the Yorkshire Dales

I Love purple

I Love sky blue

I Love my lovely house

I Love my warm, cosy snuggly bed first thing in a morning in winter

I Love the flowers and trees in my garden

I Love listening to birds sing

I Love poppies

I Love rhododendrons and azaleas

I Love wine! (anyone who knows me well will vouch for this)

I Love coffee first thing in a morning – especially on a weekend when I drink it in bed

I Love curries

I Love Spanish tapas

I Love walking
I Love dancing
I Love writing and being creative
I Love meeting new people
I Love the internet
I Love my new central heating boiler!!
I Love the plumber who came out and fitted it
I Love the smell of my children
I Love the smell of fresh cut grass
I Love music
I Love the sound of Jon's velvety voice (sorry to embarrass you again Jon!)

Because I have come at this journey from a spiritual angle I began to think about all the times that the word 'love' is used in religious scriptures. The word took on a whole new meaning for me in the context of what I had read time and time again at school.

I always thought love was a bit of a 'soft' emotion to have but actually it is the most powerful emotion you can have and connects you directly to the Universe/God/Source/Your Higher Self.

I could see the links between following your intuition (which is when you are receiving inspired guidance from a higher source) and following your heart.

As soon as I started following my heart and my intuition, my life became much happier and more fulfilled and I attracted wonderful people into it. I was doing things I love, with people I love and my spirits were lifting.

I still had a lot of things and a certain person in my life that I didn't love but I was tipping the balance and this was a first big step for me.

Tipping the balance of love I was giving out in my thoughts was beginning to magnetise more things into my life that I loved. This motivated me to really take some control over my feelings and to be very conscious of what I was thinking about at any given moment.

This does sound a bit exhausting but it is like any new skill we learn. I moved from being consciously incompetent about thinking loving thoughts, to being consciously competent and now it is firmly embedded in my unconscious. I am UNCONSCIOUSLY COMPETENT IN LOVE! – RESULT

For me the 'love' brought together the new techniques I was adopting around gratitude and happiness.

It was like a 'supercharge' to my daily routine of thinking about things I was grateful for and took my frequency to the next level.

The little mantras I was chanting whilst out walking and the words I was putting in my journal became more and more powerful.

"I love Jon because he makes me so happy in every way. I am truly blessed and grateful to have him as my wonderful funny, hubby"

"Ben makes me so happy when he is home. I am so grateful for his wonderful sense of humour and I love it when he makes me laugh out loud."

"I love chatting to Liv about all her theories on the state of the world. I am so grateful she is such a bright and thoughtful girl and it makes me really happy that she shares her thoughts with me"

"I love Friday nights when we sit down with a glass of wine and a curry. I am so grateful we have enough money to treat ourselves in this way as it gets the weekend off to a wonderful happy start."

"I am so grateful that I have strong legs and can walk because I love being out in the fresh air and with nature. It makes me so happy!"

"I love visiting Robin and Sue as we always have such a relaxing, happy time. I am so grateful they live near the seaside and we get to stay there regularly"

"I love my best buddy Kathy because she is such a special lady. I am so grateful she is my friend and I feel very blessed"

As I am writing this – I am actually getting tingles all over. A good sign!

Just going back to my comment earlier about writing thank you letters. Have you ever written a letter to someone to thank them just for being the person they are and what you love and appreciate about them?

I certainly hadn't – although Jon and I do write some pretty soppy (I mean loving and thoughtful) stuff to each other in Christmas/Birthday/Valentine cards. The kids have also adopted this approach and it is such a wonderful thing to read their cards. They actually have taken on more importance than the presents we receive from them and I think that says a lot about what is important in life.

I actually finish this book with the cards I received from Ben and Liv this Christmas which told me so much about how I had conquered my challenges and come out a better, stronger person (try not to peek...................I bet you were tempted weren't you?!)

So I want to finish this chapter with three letters I wrote to special people in my life during the early days of my 'mindful' development and learning to appreciate the important things in life.

I didn't give these letters to the people concerned at the time I wrote them as I was still early on in my journey and admit to feeling a little unsure about giving them such heartfelt letters out of the blue. So instead I'm going to go public on them now, because these people deserve to have their wonderful support acknowledged to the widest possible audience.

Dear Jon

I just wanted to say a massive thank you for being such a wonderful man.

The list of things I want to thank you for is huge and almost endless but here are some of the things that immediately spring to my mind.

You are a kind, caring and thoughtful man.

You are so funny and make me laugh.

You are a brilliant dad and the children absolutely adore you.

You have always been there for me in the good times and the bad and I am honoured and blessed to be your wife and soul mate.

Thank you for all the wonderful meals you have cooked for us; all the holidays you have organised and then got us there safely; all the love you give to me, Ben and Liv.

You truly are a wonderful, special man and I love you with all my heart and gratitude.

Loads of love

Viv


Dear Mum

Thank you so much for the warmth and love you have given me consistently throughout my life.

You are the best mum in the world and provided me with a stable, loving and happy start to life.

I admire you so much and have followed your lead in how I have brought up Ben and Liv.

You are so good at listening and seeing the common sense in all situations. I am so grateful for our Tuesday night chats which really help me rationalise things in my mind and see things in perspective.

Thank you for all the support you have given me throughout my life and in particular your recent love and support for which I am eternally grateful as it has helped keep me on my path.

You are such good fun and so kind, caring and loving and I am so blessed and happy to have you as my mum.

I love you so much.

Viv


Dear Kathy

You are such a special lady and I am truly blessed to have you as a friend.

You were meant to come into my life when you did and I have always strongly believed that we are soul mates, traveling this amazing journey together hand in hand.

I am so grateful to you for being there when I have needed you and for your unconditional kindness.

I will always remember the support you gave me when dad died, both emotionally and practically on the day of his funeral.

The biggest thing I must thank you for is that you have 'explained' to me. You have got me on the right path in understanding the Universe and the power of my thoughts and spirituality.

Thank you for explaining earth angels because that has helped me realise I have an important life purpose on this earth and has given me the courage to follow that path.

Thank you for introducing me to meditation and the Secret as it has moved me to a whole new level of mindfulness and gratitude.

Love ya hun!

Viv

Writing this chapter has just been wonderful and made me feel so happy and emotional (in a good way). I hope that in me sharing some of these things it will help you to plan a little strategy on harnessing happiness, gratitude and love.

---

### View from the Ground

Pessimistic? I think a fair observation of my former self (and on the occasional Monday even now) would be as a realist. If I had consumed half of the contents of my coffee mug / wine glass, I always felt that saying it was half empty was being realistic as well as opportunistic, because some kind soul might fill it up again. Of course,

I know better now – it's half full, but seeing as you're asking, you might as well top it up.

I should also point out, I have absolute respect for Paul McKenna. The man has helped many, many thousands of people to a better life. But I was affronted – please imagine my shock to open 2 presents from my wonderful wife which (with my state of mind at the time) told me I was miserable and fat. I was then expected to happily eat birthday cake. Is it wrong of me to have serious worries here?

Anyway, back to Viv's story. This chapter can be life changing, and a lot of what is covered has had a significant impact on me – including having a daft dance to some music when no one is watching.

Actually feeling and expressing gratitude has been an eye opener. Similar to Viv, it was instilled in me from a very early age to say thank you for gifts /acts of kindness. But, this new view on life has expanded my mind to being thankful for everything, and I mean everything – starting from the minute my left leg drops out of bed at 6:00 on a work day morning.

My routine is then one of being grateful. After my morning meditation (more on that later), I have a 30 minute walk, during which I routinely think through a minimum of 10 things I am grateful for/that I love – these include my family, friends, where I live, where I work (that is, the town where my office is based), something specific that has happened (such as just attending a concert), my health etc. By the time I get home from the walk, all is good.

I am blessed to have a great drive to work and I now appreciate that – so, supported by some great music, I look at the fields, farms, hill, and such and am grateful for this start to my day.

Love? Again, like Viv, my views on love were focussed on feelings towards someone not something. I love my family, I love (some of ☺) my friends. However, I now appreciate love really is from my heart and I love so much more. Back to my walk, aside from thinking about family and friends, I also realise I love the city in which I live, I love my house, I love food – and food loves me, I love red wine – and, sorry to repeat myself but, red wine loves me, I love holidays (specifically Spain), I love Leeds Rhinos (for the uninitiated, the World's greatest Rugby League team), I love life!

Ultimately realising true gratitude and widening the feeling of love have made a massive change to my daily attitude. Being happy, very grateful, and loving with my heart turned my life around.

**Jon**

# CHAPTER 5

# Flying Through Turbulence

*"When a system is in turbulence, the turbulence is not just out there in the environment, but is a part of the organisation or organism that you are looking at"*
*KEVIN KELLY*

*"Turbulence is life force. It is opportunity. Let's love turbulence and use it for change"*
*RAMSEY CLARK*

I have always regarded myself as quite a confident flyer. In fact I really enjoy the thrill of setting off and landing and all the excitement that goes with it. However, like most people, I am not too keen on turbulence.

I think Kevin Kelly's quote just about says it all. When there is a lot of turbulence going on outside, you can pretty much guarantee there is quite a lot of turbulence going on amongst all the passengers inside the plane.

From my own perspective, it immediately highlights my vulnerability on this great big aircraft and my feelings of complete lack of control. I begin to think about my safety and security and how to protect my family members.

All sorts of 'what ifs' start flying around my mind and I get myself worked up into quite a stew. In fact I begin to feel the physical effects of fear, including increased heart rate, sweaty palms etc.

It struck me that exactly the same thing happens to us in life when we are going through turbulent times.

When I look back on some of the recent turbulence in my life, I just could not get negative things out of my mind. I used to spend an enormous amount of my time thinking about "What if I had only done it this way?" and "What if this happens or that happens?"

Looking back on it now I can see that this was all such a waste of my energy because these negative thoughts did nothing to change my situation other than to make me feel a whole lot worse about it.

Much the same as the 'black box' flight recorder gathers data on each flight – so does your mind – and I was programming mine with a whole load of negative things that were really weighing me down.

The techniques I mentioned in the previous chapter really helped get me through all this but I soon realised, it was quite a tough job to sustain when everything in my outer environment was pretty turbulent.

I actually found myself in a bit of a slump in terms of my self-healing.

The reason I am telling you this is because a lot of the things I was reading at the time very much focussed on the 'perfect' results from using all these techniques and, on top of everything else, I began to feel like I was failing in my own self-development.

I knew I had to focus my mind on positive things but sometimes it was really tough when there were still negative things in my life. I found myself 'worrying about worrying'! Why was it I could not live up to all the wonderful success stories I was reading about people who had made their millions overnight or broken free from a relationship and lived happily ever after?

I also could not understand why the Law of Attraction, which I was avidly practising, suddenly seemed to stop working and I felt myself spiralling a bit downwards again. I became almost obsessed with reading everything I could about the Law of Attraction (and believe me there is plenty!!)

and my email inbox almost crashed with the pressure of daily emails – all pretty much saying the same thing.

I just want you to know that if you do have a bit of a 'blip' on your own journey that it happened to me too and I hope that makes you feel a bit better – you are not alone in this happening. I think it is important to share this with you so you do not feel like you have failed if you have an off day or you get some bad news and start blaming yourself, thinking you have attracted this into your life.

A lot of the books I read were written by people who had been on this journey for some time and they painted the 'perfect picture' of reality in their own lives. This did actually make me feel like I was failing in my quest for a better life and I admit there were times when I really doubted what I was doing and thought about giving up and just letting life carry on around me.

But I am not the kind of person to give up and I had already enjoyed feeling happy and positive and wanted to feel more of that more of the time. I realised that the 'journey' is an ongoing one and a continual quest to develop yourself. As Ramsey Clark said, turbulence should be looked on as an opportunity and we should love it and use it for change.

I resolved to continue my quest and expand my knowledge to try and find out why things weren't working out for me. Now the Law of Attraction did work for me here because I began to receive emails about 'Why the Law of Attraction doesn't work for so many people' and it set me right back on my flight (and right) path.

It also expanded my thinking. Up to this point, I had been really focussed on trying to be 'Pollyanna' and being positive about everything. I probably got quite irritating to some people around me in fact my kids were often heard to say, "Will you stop being so positive about <u>everything</u> mum!!!!" I think they could see right through me and that some of it was a façade.

It's OK to feel negative emotions, it's natural when you are dealing with a negative situation and it occurred to me that this was one of my big problems. I was so busy trying to be positive all the time I was actually brushing all the negative stuff under the carpet and hoping it would go away. In fact what I was doing was putting it all 'to the back of my mind' and there it was festering away in my subconscious.

At this point. my knowledge on the power of the mind expanded further. I was topping my mind up as much as possible with positive things but I wasn't dealing with all the negative things that had been programmed in there throughout my life.

It's a bit like programming loads of great new software into a computer but not doing a regular virus check and locating and removing any unwanted viruses. It doesn't matter how much positive stuff you keep loading in – if there is a virus lurking it will soon affect the performance of your computer and in the worst case scenario your system will crash.

My mental system was getting a bit clogged up and I knew I had to do some serious virus scanning and cleaning.

None of us really want to rake up a load of negative memories and I admit I was a little apprehensive about opening up a can of worms if I embarked on this process, but I knew it had to be done so my journey headed off on this new path.

I resolved to discover ways I could turn negative thoughts into positive in my conscious mind (to limit as much as possible any negative stuff being programmed in) but more importantly, find a way to extract the negative programmes embedded deeper into my subconscious mind. I also wanted to understand why the Law of Attraction had stopped working as well for me.

## Choosing Which Way to Go

*In the long run, we shape our lives and we shape ourselves.*
*The process never ends until we die. And the choices*
*we make are ultimately our own responsibility"*
*ELEANOR ROOSEVELT*

*d grant me the serenity to accept the things I cannot change,*
*The Courage to change the things I can,*
*And the wisdom to know the difference"*
*SERENITY PRAYER – REINHOLD NIEBUHR*

etimes it feels like we don't have a choice. My kids
say this to me in a beseeching tone. It feels like 'life' is
t upon us and we just have to get on with it. It also often
f very unfair when you think you are a relatively good
p n and it does not seem right to be having to deal with
di lt things.

ave learned that in any situation even though you may
no able to change it, you still have a choice. And that
cho is as to how you think and feel about the situation and
ho u respond to it.

I ve developed massively as a human through dealing
with ily challenges and I know my wisdom has increased
immesurably as a result. If life was all a bed of roses,
humaity would never advance because we would all just be
floatin around happily in our little bubbles.

"No pain, no gain" is an expression that just about sums
it up and also "What doesn't kill you makes you stronger"
is ofen heard in my vocabulary.

I realised the best approach is to look at situatio
challenge, to learn and develop from and grow as a
being and a good starting point would be to try and sv
thinking on a negative situation into positive.

There are various techniques I use to deal with si
I face on a day to day basis where I give myself a
This is immediately empowering because you feel
are in control – not necessarily of the situation – but d
how you are dealing with it.

## MOUNTAIN OR MOLEHILL?

I am really guilty of making mountains out of m
Only this morning, Jon was giving me a very nice
to and telling me not to overthink and over analysy
situation.

This really does make mountains out of molehill a
lot of it is down to perception and perspective. My pepn
of a lot of situations and interactions I was in ne
X Man were probably completely different to his peron.
He does not demonstrate or feel much emotion, vas
I am a very emotional creature so my viewpoint was ays
going to be miles away from his.

We have also had very different lives, so againting
things in perspective – something that seemed like a ster
to me was just water under the bridge for the X Man.

I began to try and look at situations completely objvely
almost as if I was a bystander looking on and not emnally
attached to the situation. I played 'make believe' a pre-
tended I was an external consultant who had been s in to
sort out the current situation I was in. This helped me step
back and look at the situations I was facing a littl more
rationally.

Another technique which is used quite a bit in hypnoherapy
is to think of a situation which is troubling you. Play the
situation out in your mind almost like a film, with you playing
the main character. Then step out of the film and put someone

else in to play your character (I always choose Angelina Jolie – one can but dream!). Replay the film and watch it as an objective bystander. Turn the film into black and white and start to fade it away and make everyone's voices sound really stupid (maybe high pitched) or get them to wear silly hats or clothes. It is a quick way to stop yourself playing something over and over in your mind which then just gets worse and worse. The other great bonus is that it really makes you laugh.

Paul McKenna also talks about 'framing'. This involves putting a frame around the situation and then looking at it from different perspectives. Looking at it from a personal perspective will always make it feel stronger. Looking at it from the other person's perspective will help to understand their viewpoint and how they may be thinking. Looking at a situation in terms of today will make it feel pretty intense, but looking at it in terms of the events of the week you have had or the month or the year (or you whole life so far!) suddenly helps you to put it in perspective and bring a bit of balance to the situation.

## NEGATIVE OR POSITIVE?

I have learned a couple of really great techniques here which I mentioned earlier in the book.

The first one I use when I catch myself thinking something negative and feeling sorry for myself - "I don't want all this debt!" "I don't want this person in my life!" "I don't want this job anymore!" "I don't want this aching neck and shoulder!"

My subconscious was being programmed with all the stuff I didn't want and I remembered that it doesn't differentiate so I was just attracting more of the same into my life.

I immediately switch it to what I do want. "I want to have paid off all my creditors." "I want to be in a position where I can work with lovely people." "I want a wonderful job where I feel happy every day." "I want a flexible and supple neck and shoulder" This sounds so simple but it does really work and got me thinking about the positive things I wanted rather than the negative things I didn't want.

I think of it almost as turning around on your path. For a long time I was walking backwards looking at everything behind me and saying I didn't want it. I also kept warily looking over my shoulder wondering what I was walking towards. I was soon going to trip up if I carried on walking backwards not looking where I was going! I turned right around and started facing forwards, towards what I really did want and when you focus on all the good stuff you want ahead of you it gives you the impetus to move towards it.

I'm happy to report that I now work with wonderful people in a job I love and I have wonderfully supple and flexible neck and shoulders. I am also chipping away at the creditors!

The other technique I learned to use was equally as simple and equally as effective. In any situation that is thrown at you – instantly think "GOOD!" I found that saying this one word instantly got my mind to work on what was good about the situation. It is almost like your brain cannot help itself. If you say "GOOD!", it has to think of something good about the situation and this immediately makes you feel better. I also find it quite empowering, because saying this word seems to make you feel back in control of the situation. It almost makes you feel like "Yes, that is what I wanted to happen because it is good for me in this way."

For a little while I had a post-it note stuck on my laptop and whenever any potentially negative situation arose I just said 'GOOD!" It definitely lightens things up a bit.

## REACTING OR RESPONDING?

A while ago, I would not have thought there was much difference between these two words – but I know through painful experience there is a massive difference.

Reacting to a situation is an 'instant' thing. You don't really think about it, you just react and it will be charged with all the emotion and beliefs that you have built up over your lifetime in similar situations.

I used to spend nearly all my time reacting to things the X Man said and did, and all it ever did was just escalate the situation and make me feel worse and worse.

I have now learned to respond. Responding is a much more considered approach. It gives you time to think and to use your rational mind. It also gives you time to look at the situation and try to turn your thinking round into positive.

I remember reading something about how to deal with a situation that has arisen, which feels utterly terrifying. This advice was to leave it for three days before doing anything. Clearly there are occasions when you can't use the 'three day' trick (for example if a huge bus is hurtling towards you!) but I tried it when some things happened in my business world and it honestly works. In the best case scenario, the situation gets resolved and completely disappears. In the worst case scenario you feel tons better about the situation having left it for three days. It gives you thinking and rationalising time and puts things in perspective.

## COMFORT OR TERROR?

Now this sounds like a bit of a no brainer doesn't it. In any situation we are always going to choose comfort over terror.... aren't we?

Well I learned to my detriment that choosing 'comfort' when you are going through turbulence is quite possibly the worst option you can choose.

Looking back I can see that because I do not like conflict and because I was interacting with someone who positively revelled in conflict that I always took the 'comfort' option. This really was my downfall and I don't say that lightly. I allowed another person to completely rule the roost in everything and at the time it seemed the most 'comfortable' option was to just let that happen. I now realise that the damage that did to me and to a lot of other people around me, was significant and that this was largely the cause of a lot of my later problems and the negative situations I found myself in.

I was reacting by going into my comfort zone and I was not thinking rationally about the consequences of me not standing up for my values and viewpoint and then responding.

If I had only stepped over my 'terror' barrier, rather than staying in my 'comfort zone' with my head buried in the sand – a lot of things would not have happened that did. The more I let things happen, the more the downward spiral descended and that has been one of my very big life lessons learned.

I read about a great technique which helped me get out of my comfort zone and across the terror barrier in potential conflict situations. It is to actually think about the consequences of staying in your comfort zone and not doing something and to see that potential result as the 'terror' and not the situation you are facing right now.

This was really the point at which I started to reflect on my current life and the consequences of not doing something about it. I could stay in my comfort zone and not take any action. That would have been the easy route on a day to day basis but I certainly did not want to carry this on for the rest of my foreseeable future, just watching everything get worse in my working life. The consequences of that were almost unbearable and it jolted me into action.

For me to be truly happy and live my life purpose and dream, I had to make some massive changes. I had to step over my terror barrier and let the X Man know that I no longer wanted to work with him.

The amazing thing was that when I finally stepped over my terror barrier and had the discussion that I thought was going to be horrendous – it was nothing of the sort.

In fact it enabled us to have a rational conversation about issues we both had and for a while our relationship was back on an even keel. There is more to come on this one because, although I made a massive step forward here and was very proud of myself and relieved, there was more turbulence ahead and that was largely down to the fact that I was still dithering with my FINAL decision!

## PROCRASTINATION OR ACTION?

To a certain extent this links to the last section, but I think it is worthy of a separate heading because I realised that one of the things that really holds me back in life is 'procrastination'. I am very good at it. If there is something I don't want to do or don't feel confident doing, I will find every excuse under the sun not to do it. A great form of procrastination is checking emails. You can spend all day checking emails and get little else done, but it kept me in my comfort zone because I didn't have to make any difficult decisions or have any difficult conversations. Another great form of procrastination is 'planning'. I found that because I was losing heart and there were things going on around me that I don't like, I just slipped into my shell and would avoid anything that seemed like it might be a bit of a challenge, so would spend a lot of my day planning what I was going to do. The only problem was, that was as far as it got!

I had had so many difficult situations to deal with recently, that I had built up a whole host of negative programmes in my mind and they were predominantly fear and doubt based.

Anybody who knew me a few years ago at work would be shocked to hear this. I was a real 'go-getter' and really self-confident. I was really focussed on my personal and work goals and I went for it all the time with a confidence that I would succeed – and of course I did succeed.

The last few years had completely knocked my self-confidence and self-esteem and I could see it was really showing in my approach to work.

I had some really good days where I wrote myself a list and took action in a completely focussed way and it will be no surprise to hear that on those days I had some real successes.

Taking action meant feeling in control and I think when you are going through turbulence it is really important to feel that you do have some control over the situation. I found that taking good, measured, well thought out action made me feel much better about the situation I was in.

I have found that taking daily action towards my new life has really helped give me some hope on a day to day basis and just achieving one small action towards that goal made me feel hopeful and happy.

If I found myself procrastinating it was a sign to me that I was doing something I didn't want to do or was afraid of doing and becoming aware of this helped me to take some action. Either working on overcoming my fear of doing what needed to be done or doing something else.

## HEAD OR HEART?

A while ago I would have always gone with 'head'. In fact I did and look where it got me!

Going with your heart sounds like the soft option but believe me it is sometimes the more challenging option and it is definitely the right option.

I am now working with people I love, doing something I love and am happier than I have been in a long time and that is because I am learning to follow my intuition and all those 'light bulb' moments I keep getting these days.

When you follow your intuition you are following guidance from higher sources (or your higher self) who have your greatest good at heart. Putting this into practice has definitely led me to make the right decisions about things and in one instance actually stopped me almost inadvertently embarking on the same path I have followed with the X Man, with somebody else. My gut instinct was so strong saying 'No!!!!!!' – I just couldn't ignore it.

Go with the heart every time!

## PARADIGMS AND AFFIRMATIONS

I admit to not knowing how to pronounce the word 'paradigm' until quite recently and now I hear it a lot (its pronounced paradime for any of you who admit to not knowing either).

The easiest way to describe paradigms is to say that it is a multitude of habits programmed into your mind that control your behaviour.

Paradigms are embedded in your subconscious and are controlling you even though you do not know it and will not be aware of what they are doing!

That sounds quite scary doesn't it, but once I began to understand a bit more about paradigms I could see that I needed to do a bit more than just think positive happy thoughts and be grateful.

As I see it there are two main choices in how to deal with paradigms because they are pretty stubborn critters in terms of identifying them and then dealing with them. Going back to my computer programme analogy you can:

*Overwrite them
*Delete them

My early studies focussed on the 'overwrite' option. This predominantly involves 'affirmations'. To overwrite a negative programme you have to programme in more positive things. Most of the gurus recommend a 28 day programme of 'overwriting' with positive affirmations.

The last chapter contains a lot of the affirmations I came up with. Thinking about things you love and things you are grateful for and repeating them over and over again will eventually embed them in your subconscious mind and hopefully overwrite what is already there. If you can overcome your slight discomfort and do this whilst looking at yourself in a mirror it is even more powerful.

You can also develop affirmations about your dream future life and say things like:

"I am so grateful now that I have paid off all my debts"

"I am so happy and grateful now that I am working in a job I love"

"I am so grateful now my business is a real success"

"I am so grateful now I have found my ideal partner"
"I am so grateful now I have full health"

You can also say them about yourself:

"I am confident and self-assured"
"I am a successful entrepreneur"
"I am healthy"
"I am happy"

These are all examples of affirmations and believe me; I spent months working on this. It was pretty exhausting!

I am sure that affirmations work for a lot of people and whilst the 'gratitude' affirmations definitely worked for me, I found it very difficult to sustain these affirmations on an ongoing basis and actually became a bit bored if I am honest.

I also found that the affirmations lost their meaning even though I was trying really hard to feel the emotion and believe it (because this is also what you should do when chanting your affirmations). It's a bit like children chanting the times table. They can do it perfectly by rote but do they really fully understand what they are saying, when they are saying it? After a while, they do, when they have that little challenge of knowing instantly what 8 x 7 is – but as you can see, it does take some time.

I certainly don't want to belittle 'affirmations' as they really work for some people and they did for me in the early days. All I would say is that it is a real commitment and I almost felt like it was putting a 'sticking plaster' on the wound rather than properly healing it from within.

Perhaps it was because I was still going through a challenging time and the 'affirmations' just got caught up in all the turbulence but I knew I wasn't quite there yet.

I realised that perhaps my 'paradigms' were too deeply embedded in and there were too many of them to be overwritten so I had to go for the 'Deleting' option.

## View from the Ground

Other than being unable to take pain away from one of your children when they are ill, watching the one you love going through turbulence is one of the most difficult situations to experience. Of course, we talked a lot through the most painful time (as we talk now a lot through the happy times), but it is hard not to react.

As Viv says, the Law of Attraction is wonderful but, if taken too literally, you could be disappointed. You may sit there in a bar looking at an empty wine glass believing it to be half full and refusing another drink. Yes, sometimes your glass is empty – so get it refilled! Sometimes it may even get knocked over, so go get another one.

Sometimes, some things happen that we don't like and, as Viv has discussed, we have to find a way that suits us to deal with these things to come out of the other end bigger, stronger, happier.

Please don't think I am knocking the Law of Attraction, it was a magnificent starting point and it remains a strong point of reference, but it just needs to be taken in context.

We all have different styles and I have learned a lot from Viv on this subject and have become stronger for it and am learning to fly more smoothly in my own professional and personal worlds, which is certainly to the benefit of those around me.

Perhaps another 'wrong' way of dealing with things, which has not been discussed is 'lash or slash'. In other words, whichever way the situation was handled, someone or something got damaged. I kind of think that was sometimes my preferred way of operating, but with hindsight the only person who was really damaged was me. In acting like this I was creating my own highly turbulent situation.

However, the journey that I have been travelling with Viv has helped correct things.

All of the above resonates but 'negative or positive?' 'reacting or responding?' 'comfort or terror?' 'procrastination or action?' and 'head or heart?' all feature in my life – certainly from a professional perspective.

How many times have I looked at a project and thought I couldn't do it. Rather than really looked at it; thought about what was needed; when it was needed by; who I could enlist to support me; what other resources were available and just got on with it? How many times has someone said something which sounded critical and I have reacted, rather than thought about what was being said and actually realised it had been said for my benefit, so with a bit of thought I could have actually responded to the comment.

Hopefully you get the picture. It is all a personal choice as to how we deal with our turbulent times. Viv has discussed her learnings. You will also learn through your own experience, but the important thing to take with you is that you can learn, be stronger, and fly and then soar above the turbulence.

**Jon**

## The Here and Now

*"I do not want to foresee the future. I am concerned with taking care of the present. God has given me no control over the moment following"*
*MAHATMA GANDHI*

*"The distinction between the past, present and future is only a stubbornly persistent illusion"*
*ALBERT EINSTEIN*

When I was first planning this chapter, I called this section 'Past, Present and Future' and I was going to talk about how important it is to live in the here and now.

It is really important to live in the here and now and I am very clear on that. I spent far too much of my time thinking about all the things that had happened in the past and getting myself angry, frustrated and upset about these things all over again. What a waste of time. What's done is done. I now know to just learn from the experience and take that learning forward into my present moment (not all those horrible memories!).

I have also learned that it is definitely not a good thing to worry about the future. I know all you business planners and strategists out there might think this is a bit of a gung-ho attitude but having spent 4 years with someone who spends most of their time planning and strategizing I have discovered that at some point you really do have to take some action in the here and now.

Have a clear picture of your vision for the future and then take 'inspired action'. This means follow your heart and act on any inspiring prompts or thoughts you have. I've been doing this for the last few months and it really does honstly work. When I have asked for inspired guidance – I am often told to 'go with the flow' and 'get on the slip stream'. Interesting advice and when I am able to follow it (and not let my ego get in the way!) I find it creates a very peaceful approach to life and works very well with things seeming to appear at just the right moment.

That's about all I'm going to say on the past, present and future, even though I did originally plan to write a lot more.

Well I've decided to go with the flow and act on some inspired thoughts I received about this chapter! I have been guided (from those on high who can be quite persistent sometimes!) to actually bring my writing 'live' so what I am writing right now is in the 'here and now' of my life.

The reason I am doing this is because I am going through a bit of turbulence right now and I want you to travel along with me to see how I get through it.

I mentioned that I had realised I needed to go for the more powerful 'delete' option and that is exactly what I am harnessing now so I want to share how it goes.

I have also had a whole load of new concepts and information come my way recently which has come just at the right time. Remember I call that.............synchronicity.

I have focussed quite a bit in this chapter on the 'science' side of things but this is where it gets really quite spiritual and to be honest, from my personal point of view, this is where it gets really powerful and exciting too.

Some quite profound things are happening to me at the moment and it is as if I have been drawn back to the spiritual side of things. I am sure Jon will have his 'grounded' take on all of this in his 'View from the Ground' section!

So where am I right now? Well to be honest in quite a lot of turbulence in terms of my thoughts. In fact I have been beating myself up over my current situation and have really become quite indecisive.

The main thing that is holding me back is money. In fact it isn't the 'main' thing – it is 'THE' thing. I have financial commitments which I almost feel are freezing my progress forward with my new found happy life.

I honestly do not know what is the right thing to do and it has felt a lot like I have hit a brick wall. I really want to follow my heart and I have started doing that, but I haven't gone all out and fully committed. I feel a bit like I am dipping my toe in a lot of different waters and not getting very far as a result.

Why can't I just take that brave and courageous step and go for it?

What is it that is holding me back? I know deep down that the situation I am in is not going to change by me just hanging around and dipping my toe in every now and then. So what is really holding me back?

I have managed to stay calm, serene and happy by deploying all the techniques I have already talked about (and some I will talk about in the next chapter) but I know there is something holding me back and I know it is probably something deeply embedded in my sub-conscious that I am not even aware of.

How the heck do I bring it to the fore and 'delete' the programme?

Then, as if by magic two very new and intriguing concepts passed by my laptop.

The first was an email entitled 'Why is the Law of Attraction' not working for you?" and the second was an email advertising a book called 'At Zero' by Joe Vitale.

In addition another book appeared unexpectedly in my sights and these three things really helped me piece the jigsaw together.

## Forgiving and Releasing

*"When I let go of what I am, I become what I might be.*
*When I let go of what I have, I receive what I need."*
TAO TE CHING

*"In the process of letting go you will lose many things from*
*the past. It will be permanent, self rooted in awareness*
*and creativity. Once you have captured this,*
*you have captured the world."*
DEEPAK CHOPRA

I recently ran an Angel Workshop with Jean. Yes, you heard me right an 'Angel workshop'! Now if someone had said to me eighteen months ago that I would be running an Angel Workshop I really would have thought they had gone mad. It just shows how our life takes such interesting twists and turns and we can never really plan how it is going to pan out. Just head off in a direction, 'go with the flow', following our heart and the rest seems to be taken care of.

The workshop was amazing. It was all business people in the workshop (male and female) and Jean and I took them through a number of meditations and discussions with a view to them connecting with their angels. Pretty much everyone connected and got some messages and answers and we also had a visit from an archangel and one of the participants was given their name. She was given the name Cassiel.

The word and a bright light came to the participant just after we had done the releasing session and we looked it up in a book while we were there. Can you believe this is the archangel for Saturdays and we were running the workshop on Saturday? Everyone was pretty blown away by that one. I have looked a bit more into this and Archangel Cassiel's main duty is 'teacher' and 'spirituality' – how amazing is that given what we were doing that day. And, as if this wasn't enough, Archangel Cassiel specialises in helping you cleanse away negative feelings to help heal mind, body and spirit and helps us manifest our dreams and think beyond ourselves to become positioned on a higher spiritual plane. He came right after we had finished the releasing session.

So, I am beginning to see just how powerful it is to release – as this moves our minds onto a higher level. Whether we want to call that God/Angels/Higher Mind – I don't think it really matters – but it definitely works.

The original reason I started telling this story was because Jean had brought some books with her to the workshop and placed them around the room for people to look at. As you can see – one of them had already come in very useful! As we were tidying up at the end of the session I picked up a book and it really grabbed my attention. It is called 'The Angel Within Us' by John Randolph Price and I spotted it because it looked very much like another Angel book Jean keeps lending me (and then struggles to prise back off me!).

## Help from the Angels and a bit of meditation

I started reading the book when I got home and it had a profound impact on me. The opening chapter outlines a discussion John had with an angel where he was given an understanding that all his negative 'vibrations' (thoughts and feelings) are projected onto his Angel and they have no choice but to replay these onto the screen of our world – and it really hurts them. He was advised that he must conquer these defects so that the Angel was free to reveal his kingdom of heaven.

The more scientific amongst us would see this as negative thoughts and emotions projected onto our sub-conscious mind which in turn creates paradigms that control our behaviour. This then impacts on our outer world.

So I can see really clearly now that whichever way I look at this – it is critical to focus on releasing that negativity out of me because my life will not fully become what it should be until I do.

I know now that when I can get my consciousness to a point where it is attuned to the higher vibrations of the spiritual realm, I will experience the true nature of the angel in my life.

The book advises that to get to this level, the priority is a cleansing of the mind and heart so that all the detrimental projections (or programmes as I think of them) can be withdrawn and the energy blocks dissolve.

Now – this is a little tricky when you are going through turbulence – but what I have realised is that I should not brush it all away and try to be Mrs Happy all the time. I really need to recognise and be aware of my reactions/emotions in certain situations and bring them to the fore to be released.

For me, it really becomes powerful when I envisage that I am working on this with my angel. It feels like I have a responsibility to my angel and that I have projected some pretty harmful things onto them over recent times.

That feeling of responsibility has propelled me to really focus on this and what I have found is that the techniques that can be used for 'releasing' are surprisingly easy.

The book recommended I start by thinking of something from the past that triggers feelings of shame or self condemnation. It advises you to bring the whole scenario into full view. So I am going to do this right now. I, of course, am thinking about the last four years and of how I was weak with the X Man and did not follow my heart and my intuition. How I let things happen that completely went against my values and hurt other people, but I did not have the self-esteem to stand up for what I knew was right. I am now bringing this all into my mind and thinking of various 'scenes' where I let myself be walked all over. I am pulling up every 'sin-fear-guilt' root that I can and am now giving it to Spirit to let it be burned away.

I'm now thinking about the personality problems I have experienced. These are fear, shame, anger, confusion, jealousy, feelings of futility and impatience.

I'm now thinking of the negative appearances in my life and these are financial and legal challenges and business problems.

I am tossing it all onto the fire.

I am now completely surrendering it all and cutting the chords on all these negative things.

I am now going to bring into my awareness the dwelling of my Spirit and I am going to ask to be escorted to the particular angel I need to see. I am going to ask "What can I do to assist you in your work of manifesting perfection in my life?"

Bear with me – I'm just going into a bit of a meditation here.........................

STOP PRESS!!!

Just as I'm typing this, I am thinking about 'Ryan The Window Cleaner'. The reason he popped into my head is because I did a Shamanic Meditation reading (more on this later) for him the other day and one of the things I saw was some papers being burned. I was thinking about Ryan and that I would send him this part of my book as it might help him with a situation he is dealing with at the moment, which is on a real parallel to my own. Well, it will come as no surprise for you to hear that right at the moment I was thinking about Ryan – he called. He called to say he would like to have a go at doing the Shamanic Meditations himself and he was asking for a bit of advice. We had a lovely chat, as usual and when I came off the phone it struck me. Another 'light bulb' moment! Do a Shamanic Meditation on the above. They are so powerful and vivid for me. So here goes...............I'll be back in 30 minutes

.	....................I'm back. Wow! Another powerful one. Here's the journey that unfolded as I asked the question.

## "What can I do to assist you in your work of manifesting perfection in my life?"

I was in some woods. There was a beam of sunlight shining down on me through the trees. I was lying on a rock at the side of a stream and just letting the sun shine on my face. I sat up and started writing in an A4 notepad. I was writing for a while. Then I got up to walk through the woods. A voice said "Appreciate all the beauty around you." I started to notice every fine detail in the woods. Drops of water on the leaves; the moss on a fallen branch; the feel of a tree trunk; the sound of the birds twittering; the feel of the sun on my face; a load of blue butterflies fluttering around some flowers; a ladybird on a leaf. I was seeing everything in vivid detail. I then emerged out into open countryside and revelled at the scene in front of me. The grass looked really green, I knelt down and felt it on my bare legs and marvelled at how much abundance of grass there was and how perfect each blade was. I looked up at the sky and all the fluffy white clouds. Faces appeared in the clouds and they were all my loved ones – family and friends. A robin was on a gatepost watching and a little lamb gambolled up and pranced around me. It was like I was seeing everything through a new pair of eyes. I noticed a big hole in the ground (like the entrance to a rabbit warren). I walked down it and could smell the lovely earth and there were little rabbits popping about around me. I walked through the earth tunnel and came out on a ledge looking out over a fabulous canyon. I couldn't see any way to carry on and then suddenly this brilliant white light began to emerge from behind the hill on the other side of the ravine. It turned into this huge angel who held its hand out and I stepped onto it.

I heard the word "Trust."

The angel flew up into the air carrying me and I saw the scene from a different perspective from high up. I could see how small everything seemed from up there. We eventually landed near a ranch and there were a load of people inside a fenced off area. I walked through them and stood on a little rock. They all sat down on the floor and I got my A4 notepad out. I started reading to them and they were all listening. There was a group of people to my right dressed in brown sack cloths and they were all sniggering and pointing at me and whispering. I smiled at them and said "Come and join us. I hope it will help you." They didn't move but then people from the main crowd got up and walked over to them and held their hands out. Eventually all the people dressed in brown joined the main group.

I looked down at my A4 notepad and there were the words 'Dreams become reality.'

I carried on walking and ended up in a desert. I was following the bright light of the angel and I heard the words "Keep following us." There was a Big Red Indian Chief at the side of me and he was nodding as if to say "Yes you are doing the right thing." Then he held out his hand and there was a gold coin. I took it.

As I continued to follow the angel, the Indian Chief kept appearing and holding out his hand and each time there were more coins in it.

The angel then led me through a dark tunnel and blindfolded me. I couldn't see anything but sensed where the angel was so just kept following. The angel then said, "Follow the Light; Follow your Heart."

We came out of the tunnel and then the angel picked me up and whisked me off into the sky. We went higher and higher until I was in space amongst all the stars and looking down at the Earth.

> I then began throwing all my negative thoughts and memories into the air and they were exploding like fireworks with gold dust shimmering down. I kept doing this for a while until there was nothing left.
>
> Then I found myself gently floating down a beam of light and I landed back on the rock with the beam of light shining down on my face.

.......Well – what can I say. Some pretty powerful messages in there and I really do feel like a lot of things have been released. I also feel very protected and guided and like another weight has been lifted off my shoulders.

I will share some more of my Shamanic Meditations later in the book. They really are incredibly powerful for me and the other people I have done them for. I always come away with some brilliant guidance and a feeling of empowerment.

## Help from Ho'oponopono

Isn't this just the most amazing word? Half the challenge is working out how to pronounce it – but if you Google it you will find plenty of people saying it.

It is an ancient, mystical and (up until recently) secret Hawaiian healing method.

This technique is definitely my kind of technique because it is so easy and simple and yet so incredibly powerful. I have been practising Ho'oponopono since I first learned about it maybe a couple of months ago and the impact it has had on my overall demeanour and my ability to deal with difficult situations is just amazing.

Joe Vitale discovered this technique when he heard about a therapist who had been called to an institution for mentally ill, convicted criminals. These were seriously violent patients who had to be shackled or sedated and, unsurprisingly, there was high turnover of staff in the institution.

Dr Hew Len, was the therapist and he attended the institution but advised the doctors that his technique was quite different and they would just have to go with it. He did not see any of the patients individually. He sat in a room with their files and 'cleaned'. He didn't have his Mr Sheen out polishing – he was 'cleaning' the programmes in his own mind that he was feeling when he read what these patients had done. So all the emotion and feelings that came up in him as he read the files – he 'cleaned'. Within a few weeks, the patients he was 'cleaning' on began to be unshackled and unsedated. Patients began to be released and eventually the whole institution closed down because everyone had been healed and released.

Now that is a pretty powerful story and it got my attention so I wanted to understand more about this amazing healing method.

There are some principles of Ho'oponopono which I found a little difficult to grasp at first. The first principle is that we are all one mind – so anything we think will have an effect on others around us (even if they are thousands of miles away!). The second principle is that you are 100% responsible for everything in your life and environment. Anything or anyone that shows up in your experience is because of a programme in you that has brought that experience or person to you. This isn't just programmes in your subconscious from your own lifetime. This also includes programmes from all your ancestors. It's all there in your subconscious (and the big Universal Mind) so, as you can imagine, there is a heck of a lot to 'clean' and most of it you won't even be aware of.

I found it quite a challenge to feel 100% responsible for what was going on in my life and some of the people in it, but I resolved to go with it and see what happened.

The other challenging principle is that you are asking for forgiveness for these programmes and saying 'sorry'. Now I did find that a bit difficult. I definitely didn't feel like I should be saying sorry for some of the things and people in my life, but the more I read about Ho'oponopono the more

I understood that you are actually apologising to and asking for forgiveness from God/the Divine/your Angel/your subconscious mind/The Universal Mind – whichever one of these you feel most comfortable with.

The technique is simple and consists of saying four phrases:

"I love you"

"I'm sorry"

"Please forgive me"

"Thankyou"

It really is as simple as that. I saw a slightly extended version of each phrase and this helped cement it in my mind and fully understand who it was I was talking to:

"I love you Divine"

"I'm sorry I was not conscious"

"Please forgive me for being so unconscious"

"Thank you Divine for cleaning this programme"

I use the phrases whenever I can: when I'm out walking or driving or meditating and also when I recognise I have just had a negative thought or emotion about something. It immediately diffuses the feeling and emotion. I try to say the phrases in my head as often as I can and I feel like it has programmed itself into my subconscious and is playing on a loop.

I don't think I have ever felt this calm and relaxed. I can't explain it too well but it really does feel like my mind has been cleaned. I have an increased clarity of thinking and I put a lot of it down to the amazing healing method of Ho'oponopono.

## View from the Ground

Some would say I am addicted to Facebook. I would have said that it is more of an interest. However, on the basis that I have just had a sneaky peek at Facebook rather than adding a few thoughts from the ground to Viv's book as her deadline looms, maybe I should concede to an addiction. However, I will quote what I have just read "I've just had a lovely beef dinner at the local pub" ................. sorry, wrong quote.

Sorry a bit flippant, but what I read was "You know you're on the right track when you become uninterested in looking back." and I think this sums thing up and confirms that we really should live in the now.

Viv is right when she observes that I have a view from the ground on this section. Viv experiences things a lot deeper than I do, and therefore I listen to her in relation to her experiences with the angels. I have to be honest and say this is a little detached from my personal thinking but, and this is a big but (no pun intended), I believe every word Viv says. How can I do that? – please refer back to the section in the previous chapter on love.

Viv definitely reads a lot more than I do in relation to the journey we are on and, to be fair, the majority of my learning has been formed from our discussions – be that on one of our many walks, sat in bed on a Saturday morning, at the dining room table or whilst consuming the occasional glass of wine at the local pub.

That said, I am currently reading 'F**k It Therapy' by the brilliant John C Parkin. That is certainly helping me to release a lot of my personal challenges.

However, the Shamanic Meditations that Viv mentions have been useful for me. As you will realise,

I am a grounded soul of very straightforward proportions and therefore my experiences of Shamanic Meditations are worlds apart from Viv's. I don't get the images, the story or guidance but for 30 minutes I get release.

Like Viv, I focus on something from the past that triggers feelings of shame or self condemnation – an example would be as simple as lack of confidence, both professionally but also physically – and during the meditation constantly concentrate on being positive in those areas and ask how that will manifest. In other words move positive thoughts from my conscious to my sub conscious. I have to say this is work in progress but the work to date is positive and self-fulfilling.

The theory of Ho'oponopono is new and something I am working on. May be more on that in Viv's next book although I suspect that might have to come after her best seller on outputs from her Shamanic Meditations. I have read the draft and it's mind-blowing!

**Jon**

## Oneness and Unity

*"The God who existed before any religion counts on you to make oneness of the human family known and celebrated."*
DESMOND TUTU

*"I believe that Jesus realized his oneness with God and he showed. What he attempted to do was show the way to all of us, how to realise our own oneness with God also, so he's a precursor."*
ECKART TOLLE

I mentioned earlier that I had started to struggle a bit with the Law of Attraction. It wasn't working very well for me. In fact my situation was getting worse and the more I worried about worrying, the worse it got.

I began to wonder why all of a sudden it wasn't working for me and as if by magic I received the aforementioned email headed "Why is the Law of Attraction not working for you?"

It took me to a link of an interview with a chap called Gerald O'Donnell. I hadn't heard of him before so I was quite intrigued.

When I started listening to the audio I noticed that it was for well over an hour. I nearly stopped listening to it as I certainly didn't think I could spare an hour out of my day but almost as soon as Gerald started talking I was gripped.

Just to give you a bit of background on Gerald which I have taken from his biography on www.probablefutures.com. The reason I'm giving you so much on his background is that what follows could be pretty mind blowing for some.

Gerald O'Donnell holds a B.Sc. in Mathematics, a M.Sc. in computer Science, and an MBA. He is a certified Hypnotherapist. He was, amongst other activities in various fields, once considered one of the world's 7 best top technical commodities experts (independent advisor: C.T.A.) by Paine Webber and Bache Co.

He was approached in the 1980's by a Western European intelligence agency in order to join an ongoing program of mental Remote Viewing (sensing) of targeted locations. Advanced remote sensing (remote intuition) techniques were taught to field operatives, anti-terrorist units and other intelligence and/or commando squads. This operation had been set up to counter the activities of very well funded departments of the Soviet K.G.B. and military intelligence G.R.U. that were very advanced in their research and fully operational.

It is in the course of the successful experimental phase of the program that Mr. O'Donnell stumbled upon the fact that by using special mental techniques and training, not only was space bridged instantly, as the non-locality theorem of quantum physics (theorem of John Bell) had predicted and the Aspect experiment performed in 1982 had confirmed, but that the time barrier was as well conquered: allowing oneself to experience the perceived past and the probable future.

So I think you can see that Gerald started out from a pretty much 100% scientific angle.

Now during this interview, I was pretty blown away by what Gerald said but it all made sense. I see it linking with the Mayan Prophecy and some of the biggest messages he received were around 20.12. 2012 (which was when the

Mayan calendar stopped and people predicted this as the end of the world).

There is and has been a massive shift in the universe and it is the biggest one since humans were put on this earth.

Gerald channels messages from the Highest Source and he had received some pretty profound ones around the time of 20.12. 2012.

He advised that up until now God/The One/Source has allowed everything to be manifested on earth through the 'free will' of our conscious minds. God put us on this earth to be co-creators with each other and Himself. He gave us free will to manifest anything we wanted as long as we thought long and hard enough about it and put a bit of emotion and belief behind it.

God simply observed what was going on and what he has seen has not been a pretty picture. Gerald described it as, "He allowed the children to play without supervision."

Well now He has stepped in and is closely supervising. If humans want to manifest anything that is 'separate' (i.e not with a genuine aim for oneness and unity) it just will not happen. Some of the key learnings I got from this audio were:

We can now only manifest 'unity' with a focus on oneness

We have to focus on the desire of the One (as we are all part of the same One)

We have to focus on what is pure and unique and what does not understand separation

We have to focus on the flame in our heart and align ourselves with reality

Our manifestations must be in alignment with Source. Source is watching our hearts. If our hearts are pure the source will manifest it. This is our natural state. Stay pure of heart

We can shield ourselves from negativity by constantly connecting to Source

Focus on the inner and operate on the outer

It was like a massive wake up call for me. I could suddenly see where it had all gone wrong for me in 2013. Most of my thoughts of manifestation were about 'separateness' from the X Man. I was certainly finding it a challenge to stay pure of heart. I realised I was thinking about it in completely the wrong way.

I had to genuinely seek to manifest things, from the heart, that were focussed on 'oneness' and these should be pure.

I knew in that moment that I could not carry on working with the X Man. There could never be oneness and unity with him – no matter how hard I tried. It would be the challenge of a lifetime and I could see if I carried on trying to make things work, I would go through the same old cycle again and again. I know I was told in my first angel encounter that he was a lost soul and I could save him (but I didn't have to) and to be honest that had kept me there for quite a while as I felt a bit responsible to him.

I realised this was not helping my life purpose at all and I really did have to take definite action this time.

There was only one thing for it. I had to make that step and tell him I did not want to work with him anymore and that is exactly what I did. I cover this in Chapter 8.

Did anybody else have a disrupted 2013? The number of times I spoke to people this new year where they said they were glad to see the back of 2013. I think we all witnessed a year of massive shift (unbeknownst to most of us there was some big stuff going on out there in the Universe).

I am also aware that more and more people have had an 'awakening' a bit like I did. When I look back at that now I can see how the timing was to perfection. I got my first BIG message back in September 2012. In one connection with my dad after he had passed away, he actually said it had been part of the plan so that I would take this path. At the time I didn't tell many people about that because I felt a bit awful that dad had died to get me onto the path I am on now.

I have learned to accept this though because I am not entirely sure where I would be now if I had not started the 'spiritual journey' when I did. I had to be 'jolted' into it with something extreme in my life and I suspect that has happened to a lot of people.

I certainly know that a lot of the wonderful people in my life have had similar 'jolts' but I don't think we can have a world where everyone is getting jolted all at the same time. It would be a bit chaotic wouldn't it! But maybe that's why 2013 was not too good for a lot of people.

So I think this is why there is a slow awakening happening. I have seen it myself with the people I have told my story to and how they have reacted and how more and more 'ordinary' people are going down the spiritual path.

I actually find it really exciting and feel I have a part to play through this book and whatever plays out after it is published. I am certainly thoroughly enjoying the journey.

I wanted to finish this section with the transcript from a short video Gerald has on his website. It is the words he channelled on 31 December 2012. The video itself is amazing. I would recommend looking at it if you can.

These words do need a pretty open mind and Jon has struggled a bit with this new discovery but they resonated so much with me in terms of what happened to me in September 2012 and what I have been through since 31 December 2012 that I felt it was important they went in the book.

I certainly think it is a good piece of advice for how to live your life.

# Message from the One and Only Yeru-shalem
## December 31 2012

This is the Godliness
Man thinks God is far away when in fact
He is closer than one's breath
The negation of self is what caused man to fall so far
from its original purpose
Many have tried to interpret the Mind of Godliness
and until now most have failed in their perceptions of
the Ultimate reality
There needs to be absolutely no divide between
Creator and creatures
Nevertheless, the Creator has allowed Himself, until
now, to be subject to the mind of the creature in order
to experiment with the ultimate free will
This is not to be anymore, for the One-and-Only will
regain His Throne and engage in guiding His creatures
in order to allow for the continuation of the experiment
of this and many other Creations
You all will perceive this fact soon as The One
becomes an Eternal Permanent reality in your
consciousness, you will love yourselves in Oneness as
parts of The One-and-Only and you will love The One
for he is constantly Creating you in thoughts in His
Gigantic Imagination
And in turn you will be bathed in Eternal Love and
concern for your well-being
We are not more than One Mind separating Itself in
concepts and facets. We are all to be united soon into
this Holy perception
We shall all be completed and perfected
All will heal
Everything will be corrected

Nothing will remain isolated in thought and
perception for all will be aware of being important levels
and parts of Totality
We need not fear and trust in the process which has
just occurred, as the Totality of Creation has just turned
around from an expression of The One focussing on
and manifesting the many,
onto a phase of reuniting with the perception of
Himself, as the One - as the many focus from now
onward being the One-and-Only separating Itself so
that It can imagine Himself into different parts,
perceptions and operations
Soon major events will need to occur so that the
perception of The One becomes anchored into this and
many other realities
Soon no one will be allowed to even doubt it
The One-and-Only is gently asking his beloved
creatures to let go of their belief systems which
separate the Godliness and His Creation into distinct
realities for such is not the case
Time has come for the One-and-Only to bring all his
children home and show them a new Creation, a new
Song, a new Way
They all erred like lost sheep without a real shepherd
There will be no judgement placed upon
their former errors
Nevertheless, there will be great effort and intense
intervention so that man understands that there is but
One God, not many, One Source, not many, One Origin
not many and it is all The One-and-Only
All systems that flourished based on the dominion
and enslavement of others, shall be made to fully
disappear from the face of Creation

All beliefs which tried to portray the Godliness in
a restricted manner or negate His true reality
by introducing elements of Worship of lower
manifestations, shall fully disappear
The One will connect to receptive humans,
in order to guide their thoughts into newer forms of
manifestation of Creative energy to allow for a full stop
to so many dangerous and poisonous forms of it which
are now extensively used by mankind
and have created tremendous damage to
the fabric of this planet and far beyond
All entities that believe they can oppose the Will of
the Oneness will face the fury of the Oneness when It
manifests Its full and deepest love for all Creation
The Godliness knows far too well, for He has
experienced infinitely large numbers of Creations,
that uncontrolled competition always brings
about uncontrolled suffering
There shall not remain pockets of uncontrolled greed
and corruption; these shall all be made to implode
and be totally erased from Creation
Man will know its holy place and function within the
Holy fabric of All-that-Is and the Eternal support of its
Mother manifesting Nature for it.
Be strong and remember that real strength is found
in unconditional co-operation and love
Be gentle, for that is a sign of real strength
Be patient, for it will be your companion in
this phase as we all shift
Be kind, for you would then align with the One-and-
Only and be counted amongst the ones who will travel
the only path that can be allowed from now on
Be mindful of the power of your thoughts and the
directions of your intentions

Do not rush to judge one another; that is not
how the One operates
Never rejoice in the suffering of the part whom you
perceive as an opponent, for that part is but yourself
showing you often a misguided choice
Nothing exists in a vacuum; no reality, no perception,
no matter how far they seem to operate from yours
at the level of the One-and-Only there is not
distance nor any sense of location
Everything is interconnected
Everything affects each other
Everyone and everything is One
Understand that if you do so forget that very notion,
events will then be made to exist in your reality who will
remind you that no other is 'another' far away; so that
his or her fate and sense of happiness shall become
your fate and sense of happiness. Remember this
Soon only the Song of Love will be heard
The cacophony of all others shall not
even remain a memory
You are all invited to partake in that Song – the only
Song there really is, was and will ever be, at the level of
the One-and-Only Being there Is
Remember that under and behind every single event
you will see manifested from now on lies a deeper
meaning, reality and lesson
Try to see it and integrate it so that soon only
beautiful realities shall wash upon your shores
Soon warring factions and opposing ideas shall
embrace each other for they shall have no choice
remaining, as the effects of conflict will be so deeply felt
that no one will want to revisit such
Do not be afraid to proclaim your faith in unity
and love and show it to everyone and everything.
Sing only that Song

Remain holy in your path. Set an example
Walk proudly the road of unity and you shall
be rewarded for it
This is the final end and completion to
the era of conflict
This is the real beginning of Love and Creation
There is no turning back possible – that
will not be allowed
Stay focussed on Love and Love will manifest in
your life. You shall always be taken care of if you
do so by the One-and-Only
Ask strongly for the healing of your soul,
your mind and your biology and if you operate
in the the new atmosphere and fragrance of Oneness,
you will be answered
Nothing, nor anyone can impede the new Creation,
for it is fully engaged now; no lower force would
want to test Infinite Love manifested
Remember you are all One
That is all you can be
Therefore love yourselves and always try to bring
happiness to your selves, for in that act you bring
happiness to the totality
This Will Be All

# Life Lessons Learned

*"It is impossible to live without failing at something unless you live so cautiously that you might aswell not have lived at all"*
JK ROWLING

*"We are not human beings having a spiritual experience. We are spiritual beings having a human experience"*
PIERRE TEILHARD DE CHARDIN

This Chapter really is proving quite cathartic for me. It is almost like I am getting some really strong messages as I work through it and I am so glad I followed the guidance to write this chapter 'live' and in the here and now.

I hope it is helping you as much as it is helping me.

Here is another section which I didn't originally plan on putting in this chapter.

Today I had a major turning point. I am sure Jon will have something to say about me hitting another 'turning point'. Apparently it is my favourite phrase at the moment. Perhaps a reflection of the massive internal change I am going through right now but I guess if I keep hitting all these turning points I am in danger of going round and round in circles! So I am now changing the word to 'revelation' and making a conscious effort to move forward.

So...today I had a massive revelation! My mind works in a really interesting way these days. I seem to get a little seed of a thought and then it grows and grows. Related information seems to come at just the right time in little jigsaw pieces and then all of a sudden the jigsaw pieces all come together – the picture is complete and that is when I have my turning point – sorry Jon! – 'Revelation'.

A while ago I read something about not beating yourself up over past life mistakes and feeling all those negative feelings but looking at it as 'What lesson have I learned?'

From a spiritual perspective this is really important and writing this chapter about releasing, forgiving, oneness and unity has really brought it all together for me.

For some reason today the Brian Weiss book I mentioned earlier, 'Many Lives Many Masters' popped into my head and I remembered towards the end of the book when Brian was communicating with the Masters that he was told the reason his patient was channelling them was for Brian's benefit, not his patient's. They were getting an important message across to him which was that our souls come back here if there are lessons to be learned from our previous lives/ ancestors. It was his job to get this message out to the world and he did it through his book. Even though (like me) he felt a little uncomfortable about others possibly ridiculing him because of this profound experience.

This led me on to think about the Ho'oponopono method and how Joe Vitale had said we need to 'clean' not just bad programmes from our current life but also from our previous lives.

I then moved on to think what I might have done in a previous life and/or this current life where I clearly hadn't learned my lesson or achieved my life purpose and I had been sent back to do this.

I remembered back to my very first dialogue with an angel where I was told I was being tested and had to be strong because I had the important role of helping people get on with each other.

Perhaps in a previous incarnation, I was not very good at getting on with people and rubbed a lot of them up the wrong way!

I have also had a number of occasions and strong thoughts recently that I had a job in a previous life of helping people to heal through spirituality and that I was either punished for it or didn't do it in quite the way I should have done.

I am sure you are a bit intrigued here and wondering why I know these things. Well it has kind of come out of me during some of the releasing things I have been doing and I am almost starting to have memories. Very vague but they link with a lot of things I realise I now have in my subconscious, which I understand now has been affecting my thinking and behaviour.

I will give you an example of a scenario to hopefully illustrate how I have started to piece together some of the things that have been locked in my subconscious. It might help you to reflect back over your life and pull together your jigsaw pieces.

This might be a bit of the Richter scale for some of you in terms of what I have learned, but please approach these next few paragraphs with an open mind.

I can remember when I was a little girl I was fascinated with ghosts and the spirit world. I had a book which almost dropped to pieces I read it so much.

I do not remember too much about lessons at school – but there is one lesson I vividly remember because it made my blood run cold. We had been talking about torture in mediaeval times and I had coped just fine with the rack and the iron maiden and people being chained to walls and lashed. Then there was a picture of a witch being drowned. There was something about that picture that almost brought back a memory for me.

I have three very mild phobias. One is moths (not sure where that came from but I have learned to overcome it with two children who also hate moths – interesting one that!), the other is claustrophobia and the final one is being underwater or fear of drowning. Not sure if there is a phobia for that – in fact – bear with me again, I'm just going to

Google it..................got it – it's called 'aquaphobia'. Interestingly, it states that this is usually combined with a fear of swimming but I don't have that – in fact I love swimming. I just have a phobia of drowning and being trapped underwater.

It is more to do with me not being able to breathe and I think this links with the claustrophobia because it is more the fear of being trapped in a tight space and not being able to breathe that scares me.

I have had a number of recurring nightmares about being underwater and not being able to breathe and if there is anything on the television where someone is trapped underwater I have to turn it off. I also remember recently hearing about 'waterboarding' and almost being able to 'feel' how the other person would be feeling.

My lovely friend Jean is convinced I was a witch in a former life (thanks Jean!). A while ago that might have offended me but not now. I appear to be very open to the spirit world. There is a lot that has happened recently that has reinforced this including the experience I have when doing Shamanic Meditations (which apparently is pretty powerful) and also what happened when I was attuned to give Reiki (more about that later!)

Jean believes that I have had these 'gifts' in previous lives but they have been suppressed (being drowned is a good way of suppressing someone!) and/or I have misused them for my own gain. I feel a bit bad about that bit but do actually think it is true. I believe I might have experienced some of the darker side of spirituality in a previous life. Pretty cathartic stuff!

So now I am back as nice Viv (hopefully that is what people think of me) to rectify my previous misdemeanours and failures and do what my soul is here to do, which seems to be to help people heal and get on with each other.

When Jean gave me the Reiki attunement – I had a moment where I started crying. I had this overwhelming feeling that I had tried to do something 'big' in a previous life and had failed – either because I had been stopped in my tracks or that I had chickened out of it.

This is really interesting because another thing I have learned about my possible subconscious blocks is that I have a fear of success. Looking back I can see how this has really held me back. The number of times I think to myself "You can't do that Viv!" and yet everyone else seems to think I can. It also links to my discovery of my lack of self-esteem and how things that have happened to me recently have almost reinforced them.

Something came across my radar recently where you had to think of just one word to describe yourself. The absolutely best word to describe yourself. This sounds really easy but when you can only use one word you really do have to think very carefully about it. The word I came up with was 'inspiring'.

The reason I came up with this word is because I have realised that I get my biggest kick out of inspiring other people. I get even more of a kick when they tell me I have inspired them and I am getting a lot of that recently since I started on this spiritual journey.

This really is quite cathartic for me (maybe that can be my new word Jon – I've used it twice already in this section!). I am really beginning to discover what I am here for and it is to help people get on with each other by inspiring them.

I have also realised that I might actually have learned my life lesson in this life. It is quite difficult sticking your head over the parapet when you regard yourself as pretty ordinary. It also appears I might have been killed for it in a previous life and that is enough to put anyone off! There is a risk of ridicule when you start talking 'spiritual' but I know I have been gently nudged to become more open and honest about my experiences. I have also been massively encouraged along the way by the wonderful people I have around me and

I realise this has been higher powers putting all this support in my path to help me grow in confidence.

I am no longer fearful of success. In fact I hope this book is a best seller because I know I have been tasked with writing it and I sincerely hope it is going to benefit many many people.

There are two people who have helped me more than anything in overcoming my fear of success and slight concerns regarding opening up about my experiences. They are also the people in my circle who are quite the most counter intuitive in terms of someone you would expect to embrace all this spiritual stuff and they are Jon and 'Ryan the Window Cleaner'.

There is a definite reason why I have been guided towards Jon joining me in this book (mainly thanks to Jean and persistent messages from on high). I am also absolutely and utterly convinced, without a shadow of a doubt, that Ryan was brought into my life to show me just what can happen when I am brave enough to talk to someone I don't know about my spiritual experiences. It has had a deeply profound effect on Ryan and in turn his amazingly positive reaction has had a deeply profound effect on me. Thanks Ryan. You are a star!!!!!

So looking back into my past lives and beginning to understand those, has helped me see the really big picture in terms of why I am here and what has been holding me back.

I also know that I have definitely learned some lessons in this life time and it has been to do with the choices I made in business. When I have been doing the 'releasing' exercises and bringing up all my issues I have also received messages about 'what lessons have I learned'. Jean uses the phrase a lot about 'repeating life's patterns' if you do not learn your lesson first time round. She used it in terms of the X Man but it got me thinking about my own life.

It really struck me this morning and here is an email I sent to Jean.

This morning I have been thinking about my life lessons learned.

One of them was I have learned not to be impressed by offers of money and promises of riches.

I have done this twice. Once with the X Man and before that with my previous business. Both times I left the business to the person making all those promises, because they did not resonate with my values and made me unhappy.

Jon reminded me today that I have learned my lesson. The X Man's recent talk of investment made me realise there were more important things than money. i.e. my own health, happiness and mental wellbeing.

The other recent offer of investment for People Help People was another little test and I know now I have learned my lesson.

It was definitely like a 'light bulb' moment (or maybe it was a revelation, a turning point or cathartic Jon? – probably all of them!). I realised I had broken the pattern of my life twice in the space of a few months and that showed me just how far I had come on. The temptation of thousands of pounds had been put before me twice. On both occasions it made my heart sink. Now that might sound a bit strange, but it told me that I am now following my heart not my head and I have let my head lead the way for far too long with pretty disastrous consequences.

I've actually been given a third shot at it in this lifetime and I really do appreciate that – thankyou Universe! That also tells me that what I am here for IS really important (as I was told by the angel right at the beginning of all this). Someone up there must have been thinking, "When is she going to learn her life lessons?!" but I know I have got it and it has literally just happened to me over the last couple of days and it is lovely to share this with you. It is completely liberating!

I have also learned to follow my heart (ALWAYS!) and to believe in myself and my ability to be successful in my own right.

Phew!

I hope you have found this chapter useful if you are going through turbulence in your life right now.

The things I have learned during this period and shared with you in this chapter have helped me immeasurably and I am nearly there. I have stayed on the 'slip stream' and 'gone with the flow' as I was very strongly guided to do and I feel I am now coming out the other side of the turbulence with so many great gifts and wonderful people around me.

If I was to summarise how to get through turbulence:

Live in the Here and Now and appreciate all that wonderful nature around you. It really is phenomenal when you stop to properly look at it and be in it.

Forgive and Release – holding onto the past is not good if it is negative. If you are not forgiving of yourself or others you are saying you owe something or someone owes you. It is psychic debt and that is not good.

Stay Happy – find whatever it is you can that makes you feel happy and focus your energies in that direction. A great starting point is by thinking about what you love in your life and by counting your blessings.

Learn Your Life Lessons – do not beat yourself up over mistakes – we all make them and that is how we grow. Just look back and think. What can I learn from that experience? That is what we are here for.

---

## View from the Ground

I am sure you will have picked up that this chapter has been a 'light bulb' moment, a revelation, a turning point, and a cathartic experience for Viv.

This last section is, by its very nature, deep and covers many things that are above ground level but have

---

been very meaningful for Viv. The books and the sources that are referred to have supported Viv on her journey and have provided real clarity. As Viv has identified some aspects are a little clouded for someone on the ground, but again, that does not mean I have not picked out what works for me and used it in my continuing journey.

I love the J K Rowling quote and make no apology for repeating it. "It is impossible to live without failing at something unless you live so cautiously that you might as well not have lived at all." Perfect words from an inspirational person and really does emphasise the point on life lessons learned.

It is absolutely right that we should not beat ourselves up when we make a mistake. But we must learn and be stronger for it. The example Viv has given of her life lesson learned is powerful and appropriate and together we will move forward stronger and more successful as a consequence.

I did have a little chuckle when I read Viv's comment about her not believing she can do something. Not in a funny way, but just that it's so Viv. It's only now that she understands her true ability and what a gift she has. Perhaps she has failed in a previous life, but one thing is for sure – she will not fail in this. Quite the opposite.

Inspiring is an appropriate word for Viv – she inspires me every day. Perhaps I should tell her more often.

Viv has also made reference to Jean and Ryan – both of whom have been important sources of inspiration for her, for entirely difference reasons. I hear a lot about Jean and Ryan, and others in Viv's expanding collective, and would like to add my sincere gratitude for their part in her rise to completeness.

**Jon**

# CHAPTER 6

## Flying Skills

*"You will begin to touch heaven, Jonathan, in the moment that you touch perfect speed. And that isn't flying a thousand miles an hour, or a million, or flying at the speed of light. Because any number is a limit, and perfection doesn't have limits. Perfect speed, my son, is being there."*
*RICHARD BACK – JONATHAN LIVINGSTON SEAGULL: A STORY*

*"Don't believe what your eyes are telling you. All they show is limitation. Look with your understanding. Find out what you already know and you will see the way to fly."*
*RICHARD BACK – JONATHAN LIVINGSTON SEAGULL: A STORY*

I think these quotes are perfect. I admit I have not actually read this book but I have heard a lot about it and it is definitely on my reading list.

Throughout my whole journey there have been a number of skills I have picked up on the way which are now a constant in my daily practice and have become a way of life for me.

I do think that these three skills alone would really help anyone through challenging times because they get you right back to basics and to a level of clarity and 'pureness'.

They connect you to your soul and we are after all – 'spiritual beings having a human experience'. The human experience is sometimes a very challenging one for the soul, so being able to connect to your soul is a good – and very powerful - thing.

I had read somewhere that in terms of our souls learning life lessons, being on earth and being a human is quite the biggest challenge. I can certainly relate to that over recent years! I am sure many of you can, but coming through these challenges does help us to grow as individuals and I have learned to accept life's challenges as being put before me to help me grow.

The skills I am about to discuss are ones that anyone can learn and practice and that is why I love them so much.

They are the most natural things in the world (or Universe) and I would highly recommend that you give them a go. The first takes a bit of practice; the second requires others to get you started and the third is easy.

STOP PRESS!

Just as I am proof reading this chapter, I have been to visit Amanda at home. She has just had a pretty major operation and lives on her own, so Jon and I popped round to see her and help out. Can you believe as we were sat chatting, my eye was drawn to the dressing table in her bedroom and there – as if by magic – is "Jonathan Livingstone Seagull – A Story." I can now say I have read the book and confirm it is inspiring.

Synchronicity at its best!

# Meditation

*"Meditation is all about the pursuit of nothingness.
It's like the ultimate rest. It's better than the best
sleep you've ever had. It's a quieting of the mind.
It sharpens everything, especially your appreciation
of your surroundings. It keeps life fresh."*
HUGH JACKMAN

*"Meditation is painful in the beginning but it bestows
immortal bliss and supreme joy in the end."*
SWAMI SIVANDA

I rather like Hugh Jackman (sorry Jon!) so I was delighted when I found this quote from him about meditation.

This actually takes me to my first point. I had always seen meditation as something done by Buddhist monks or 'hippy tree huggers' (sorry again to the 'hippy tree huggers' – you will find later in this chapter that I am pretty much there with you now).

However, in my recent journey, I have discovered that so many people do it and it is now moving quite swiftly into the corporate world where all those stressed out chief execs are realising the power of this very simple tool for themselves and also their workforce.

I must admit when I was first introduced to the concept of meditation, I was a little sceptical and also a little afraid. My friend Kathy (the 'explainer') had kept mentioning it to me and I had politely turned down the concept.

So why was I sceptical? Well like most sceptics, I hadn't actually tried it, so I was not really in a position to judge it.

Why was I afraid? It felt a bit like messing with your mind. Also, because I had experienced some quite spiritual encounters I was more than a little concerned as to what would happen if I 'opened up' my mind as I thought I might let a load of demons in and become possessed. I know that sounds a bit extreme but I am sure other people have felt the same.

Anyway, Kathy gently persisted and in the end got me where she knew I couldn't refuse. She was running a session on meditation through the wellbeing centre she worked at. It was the first time she had done it and she needed my moral support. I couldn't say no!

So, I headed to the first class with a certain sense of trepidation but also knowing it must be OK if Kathy was doing it and I would be in safe hands.

I have to say I thoroughly enjoyed two hours of being relaxed, peaceful and clearing my head of all the 'chit chat' that goes on in it on a daily basis. Not once did we sit cross legged and chant 'om' (although this is a good technique too!). We laid down on the floor with our heads on a cushion and covered in a nice fleecy blanket.

We were taken through a number of different meditations and I came out of there feeling like a breath of fresh air had just swooped through my mind. I felt completely relaxed and at peace and my mind just seemed so clear.

There is a lot you can read on the powerful benefits of meditation from some real experts so I won't go through the technical detail here. I will give you my layman's take on meditation and how it has helped me.

Much the same as any new skill (and as Swami Sivanda highlights in the above quote) it is a little bit painful and challenging when you first start doing meditation. Your mind has this amazing knack of 'going off on one' when you are trying to relax and you find all sorts going through your head but please do persevere because it soon becomes very natural.

I haven't quite got to the realms of the Buddhist monks who can meditate in silence for hours but I can certainly move into a meditative state pretty quickly these days and keep my mind clear for a good length of time.

So here's my little journey in meditating.

## Breathing

This is one of the fundamentals of meditating. Think about your breath when you are really nervous or anxious about something. It becomes very shallow and very rapid. Now think about your breathing when you are completely relaxed. It becomes very deep and really slows down.

If you remember back to the section about our subconscious, I mentioned that the subconscious mind runs the functions of all your vital organs (heart, liver etc). Your lungs are also a vital organ and, in the main, your subconscious runs this too through our breathing. Think how many times we breathe each day and most of the time we aren't even conscious of it.

Now, the exciting thing is that we can 'consciously' control our breath. It is the only one of our vital functions that we can fully control. So if you are feeling a little panicked and your breath is getting shallow and fast and you become consciously aware of it you can slow it down.

Our breath became shallow and fast because something caused us to have feelings of fear and the subconscious mind thinks we are either running away or fighting some-thing. Now that is great if we are running away or fighting something but in today's modern society that doesn't happen too often.

It is not good for our bodies to breathe for too long in a shallow and rapid way, so we have to try and get our bodies back to a state of relaxation and that is where conscious breathing comes in.

I have learned that this is a fundamental part of meditation and relaxation and anyone can do it.

I find that as soon as I focus my mind on deeper, slower breathing a couple of things happen. First of all I feel more relaxed. The 'out' breath is definitely a good way of feeling your body completely relax. The second thing is that I am so focussed on my breathing and slowing it down that the thing in my mind that has been bothering me seems to disappear. My mind has been completely distracted with the breathing.

Breathing is so easy to do (which is a good job really!) and I use this technique of breathing deeply and slowly whenever I am feeling anxious. If I can close my eyes at the same time then all the better – although clearly I do not do this when I am driving!

In terms of breathing deeply, I also discovered that most of us breathe way to shallowly. You should actually use your stomach to breathe. Now that sounds a bit strange. Our lungs are in our chest so surely we should breathe from our chest but healthier breathing starts right at your stomach. The way I learned to do this was to lie down with my hands just touching across my stomach. As I breathed in I inflated my stomach so that my fingertips parted.

It's not a very good look for us ladies when we are wearing tight dresses but if you can do the 'stomach inflating' most of the time you are breathing right.

## Guided Meditation

In the early days, when I was learning this new technique, I found it almost essential to do 'guided meditation'. What this means is that you listen to someone else telling you what to do. They will take you through the correct process to gradually relax you and then gradually bring you back out of that relaxation and will help you with your breathing techniques. This is what I did with Kathy's class and there was also lovely music playing in the background which helps you to relax even more. I also discovered a wealth of guided meditations on the internet that you can download. Some are free downloads (although sometimes they are just a taster and annoyingly cut off just as you are getting into the vibe!) others you pay for and to be honest I think the paid for ones are well worthwhile.

I particularly like the Chakra meditations (which help you focus on opening up your chakras) and the 'body scanning' ones which get you to scan your body from the tips of your toes to the top of your head and focus on each part to check if it is holding any tension and then consciously relax it. There are also some meditation audios that are just music and these help you to relax and if you are fairly well practiced in meditation you will also be able to do a deeper meditation.

After nine months of meditating regularly, I have got to the stage where I can do some pretty deep meditations with just the aid of some music. One of these in particular is Shamanic Meditations and you have already seen an example of what I experience when I do them. I will be covering more of that later in this section.

## Stillness of Body and Mind

This is a pretty challenging one, but one that you can do with practice. It completely clears your mind of everything and helps your concentration skills massively. It also helps you to become very aware of your body and I have had some quite amazing experiences with this.

I did this technique in the very early days of my meditation journey so it can be done by non-experts but just to reassure you it takes time to build up so I didn't get any miracles straight away.

The first thing to do is find a comfy chair somewhere and sit upright with your feet on the floor but in a nice relaxed way. Close your eyes and concentrate on keeping your body completely still. It sounds easy. But try it!

I managed five minutes the first time I did it. I then quickly managed to increase it to ten minutes, then fifteen and amazingly eventually to thirty minutes. That is about my limit but when you do this you become so aware of every part of your body.

Because I was focussing so much on keeping every part of my body still, I found myself really focussing in on each bit of my body if it felt like I was going to move it by mistake. I also found that I could actually feel some of the internal workings of my body (so things like my blood circulating and pulsing around my system) and it almost becomes hypnotic.

The other thing I found was that, because I was keeping very still, I became aware of any tension in my body. It was at the points of tension where I was feeling like I might move my body so I had to consciously relax them. So by the time I had done even just ten minutes, my body felt very relaxed.

The next level is to then keep your body completely still whilst also concentrating on keeping your mind still. Have you ever tried to think of absolutely nothing? It is really difficult. Focussing on keeping my body still really helped but I found my mind drifting very quickly and I suddenly 'caught myself' thinking about something. This is all perfectly natural and I learned that the important thing is that it raised my consciousness of what I was thinking and the technique I used was to give the thought some wings and let it gently fly off out of my mind.

I admit I have not got to the levels of the Buddhist monks who can clear their minds for hours but I have certainly got to the point where I can completely clear it for a few minutes and be very aware of when a naughty little thought starts creeping in.

I have found that since adopting this technique, my concentration levels have improved massively.

## Shamanic Meditation

This has been an absolute revelation (there I go using that word again) for me. I think we are all different and we will find our own methods of meditation which suit us and our lifestyles but for me it is Shamanic Meditations all the way.

Jean sent me a link a few months ago to some Shamanic Music and thought I might be interested to give it a go. The music was called "Shamanic Journey – Deep Theta" by Niall.

I clicked on the link and had a bit of a read about what Shamanic Meditation was because I hadn't come across it before.

Shamanism is the path to knowledge and also to healing of the soul.

The idea of a Shamanic Meditation is that you go on a Shamanic journey to discover some answers. Throughout the meditation you travel a journey, meet various people and have various experiences. You are given messages that will help you in your life.

Within this journey you are connecting quite powerfully to the spirit world and it is one of the oldest ways in which humans can connect directly to Creation.

The music I listen to is lovely and has a very powerful background drumming beat. This is designed to take you into a deep 'theta' state which is almost like having a dream but you are awake.

When I do the Shamanic Meditation it is like I am having a very vivid dream. It is almost like watching a film where I am initially watching myself and then as I get into a deeper theta state I actually become part of the dream and see everything through my own eyes. I have learned so many powerful things from these meditations and have a whole collection of them. In fact, that is my next book – 'Shamanic Journeys of Discovery – Messages for The World and Humanity"!

I have already given you a taste of a meditation I did in the Flying Through Turbulence chapter and it gave me some very powerful answers. I have also started doing them for other people and asking questions on their behalf and the results have been astonishingly accurate for people. This feels like such a gift for me to be able to do this to help other people and I have certainly helped people get answers to pressing questions and in some instances 'closure' on something tough that has happened in their life.

The way the meditation works for me is that I start out listening to the music and try to completely clear my mind and relax. I go into the meditation with a question and the request that I would like to 'Know' something when I have completed my journey. So I think about what it is I want to 'know' and repeat this phrase in the early stages of the meditation.

I start by imagining me in a really nice restful scene and eventually I start walking towards some type of door (often someone or an animal has got my attention and I follow them). This 'entrance' has ranged from big wooden doors through to rabbit holes and vortexes in space. I always then end up in a dark tunnel with a light shining at the end of it. The entrances are never the same, but I know that when I have gone through the tunnel and into the bright light that I am entering the spirit world. I cannot even begin to explain how this all works but what I do know is that I am connecting to the spirit world at a very deep level and I get some pretty profound and often unexpected answers.

They have helped guide me through the past turbulent times and have given me a confidence and a feeling of empowerment to deal with challenging situations.

I'm going to share one of these with you now (and there will be one more later in the book).

---

**Knowing if I have any subconscious blocks that are sabotaging my success and how to overcome them.**

The scene was a huge waterfall with a pool at the bottom of it. There were flat rocks all around the pool and I was lying on one basking in the sun. I looked up and around me was a really colourful scene. Loads of

---

Red Indian women all washing clothes in the pool and scrubbing them on the rocks.

I wandered over to the waterfall and had an urge to walk through it. Behind the waterfall was a cave and I walked through it. There was daylight at the end. The cave was lovely and cool and wet but I felt a bit vulnerable because I had bare feet. It worried me and I considered going back to get my shoes but I thought "No – I have to carry on NOW".

When I got to the daylight. I had to step across a small gap to carry on my journey. When I looked down there was a massive drop down into a ravine. I was worried I might miss my footing and fall down the ravine but I knew I had to carry on so I gathered my courage and leapt across. I felt really proud of myself for not turning back.

I carried on walking and the scene changed to a night time scene. There was a party going on outside and lots of laughter and chatter. I carried on walking and came to a 'hot coals' path. All my special friends and family were at the side cheering me along to walk across the hot coals (I had bare feet!!!!). I was quite scared about doing it but knew I had to carry on along the path so I just gritted my teeth and went for it. Everyone was cheering me along and I felt really elated when I did it. I believed I could do it and I did!

I carried on and ended up walking through a big open field. All of a sudden this huge tiger came running towards me looking really ferocious. The field was massive and I had absolutely nowhere to hide I felt really exposed and vulnerable and was really scared. I got my magic wand out (this has appeared in other mediations) and sprinkled gold dust all over the tiger. He turned into a real softie and we ended up having a bit of a play and I cuddled into his fur.

We then walked together and came to this huge ravine. It was a bit like the Grand Canyon. I knew I had to go across. There was a bridge to my right and I walked over to it and thought "Oh here is an easy way across" – but it was a rope type bridge and there was a lot of frayed rope on it. It looked like the easy route but a bit unstable.

I realised the only way I was going to get across was if I flew. My family and friends appeared behind me and were cheering me on again. I got myself really psyched up. Sprinkled the gold dust over myself and took a flying leap across the ravine. I soared up into the air and realised I was flying and felt completely elated. I flew around for a while just really loving the feeling.

I then knew that I had to get everyone else to do the same. So I landed back down in front of everyone and was really urging them and getting them all hyped up to do the same as I did. There were quite a few people who were nervous about it and I was really rousing everyone

"Come on!!! Let's do it together. Let's all hold hands and take that leap as one!!!"

We all held hands and went running to the edge together and then just lifted off. We all flew in formation across the countryside and everywhere we flew there was gold dust sprinkled on the land. People on the ground were looking up at us and all cheering and waving and shouting "Thank you – thankyou"

We carried on flying and then I landed at the top of the waterfall.

I stood at the top of it with my hands on my hips like a winning warrior

"I had conquered my subconscious blocks of fear and doubt!"

## View from the Ground

I had to smile when I read that Viv had always seen meditation as something done by Buddhist monks or 'hippy tree huggers' because that was always my naïve view. When Viv told me she was going to attend a meditation group run by her friend Kathy I mocked her about sitting in a group uttering 'hhhooooommmmm' with hands pointing to the stars. What a hoot I am!!!

However, with learning I decided to give it a go. Now, I may resemble a little fat Buddha doll – rather than Hugh Jackman, that's as close as I get to my perception of meditation.

I've already discussed how I use the Shamanic Meditation process and that works for me. I've landed at using this method having tried several others – through Bob Procter and Mind Valley – but Shamanic Meditation works, certainly with the music involved and Hugh Jackman, who is now my nemesis, is right – meditation is all about the pursuit of nothingness and like the ultimate rest.

I choose to meditate every morning before I go to work – as I've mentioned before. But it really is wonderful. I don't know about you, but when I wake up my mind is full of a whole host of things and the meditation just stops that in its track – clearance and de-clutter.

After a thirty minute meditation, I go out for my 2 mile pre-work work and I can put everything into perspective – as if mentally writing on a blank piece of paper.

Meditation has been a revelation and I talk about it a lot – maybe too much – but I am keen to try and guide others who I think it might help. To give back a bit of what I have learned.

**Jon**

# *Reiki*

*"The wish for healing has always been half of health."*
LUCIUS ANNAEUS SENECA

*"The art of healing comes from nature, not from the physician.
Therefore the physician must start from nature,
with an open mind."*
PARACELSUS

Talking of 'magic', I have to say that Reiki healing is a phenomenon that seems like a miracle to me.

I've briefly mentioned Reiki already in this book, in the section around energy, so won't repeat myself too much here but just a quick reminder.

Reiki is spiritual energy. The word Reiki is divided into two parts:

*Rei* – means 'sacred', 'soul' 'spirit' and 'the wisdom and knowledge of all the Universe'

*Ki* – is the life-force energy that flows through every living thing – plants, animals and humans and is even present in things like rock, metals etc

When someone performs Reiki on themselves or another person (or animal, or even plant!) they are channelling that energy with the intent of healing.

Anyone can be a channel for this energy. It is already in us but sometimes needs a bit of a top up particularly if we are at a low ebb with our own energy.

I heard about Reiki a few years ago. A friend of mine was quite spiritual and had the 'gift' of Reiki healing. I didn't really think much of it at the time and to be honest thought it sounded a bit mumbo jumbo. Even with my open mind, I was not convinced about what it did and how it worked.

My friend had said she would give me a Reiki session and all I needed to do was relax and just 'go with the flow' of whatever I was feeling.

At the time I was a busy mum, juggling my business and looking after a three year old and seven year old and I jumped at the chance of lying relaxing on a sofa for a bit, whilst someone gave me a nice 'massage'.

Imagine my surprise when my friend did not touch me during the Reiki healing session. However, the amazing thing was that I actually felt this warm glow wherever her hands were hovering. It almost felt like someone was pouring some warm liquid into me and it was spreading through my body. When my friend reached my head, I had the most bizarre sensation. The only way I can describe it is I could almost see all these electrical impulses in my head – a bit like you would imagine 'pins and needles' looks.

I felt completely relaxed after the session and my friend said, "Now make sure you drink loads of water because the Reiki will have released some toxins in you." At the time I was not a massive water drinker (I much preferred wine!) and I am afraid to say, I did not follow that advice. Needless to say, I felt pretty rough the next day and the day after (but not in a way I had ever felt rough before). I was suitably admonished and resolved to make drinking water a bigger part of my life. I now drink at least 2 litres a day.

However, after a couple of days, I began to feel the best I had done in a long time both physically and mentally. Life as a busy mum took over and I never gave it a seconds thought until fourteen years later when I began to form my friendship with Jean.

One day Jean asked me if I had ever experienced Reiki and I told her the above story. When I told her what had gone on in my head (the pins and needles experience) she immediately said, "We need to give you a Reiki attunement."

I have to say I was a little wary because I had felt a bit rough after my one and only experience but Jean, as always, was gently persistent and we agreed a date for my 'attunement'. I didn't really know what an 'attunement' was and for some reason didn't think to ask. I thought it was just another word for having some Reiki healing. Imagine my surprise when Jean explained that the 'attunement' would mean that I could give Reiki to other people.

This just felt so right at the time so I decided to embrace it and see what happened.

We had a lovely session. Jean gave me some Reiki healing first which was quite powerful and released some things (I've mentioned this previously). She then gave me the attunement which only took a few minutes. Everything felt very peaceful and calm (although you cannot help but feel peaceful and calm in Jean's presence) and I felt very serene and rested afterwards.

The idea was that I should practice 'self-healing' first for a few weeks and once I had got the hang of it I could try it on others.

That evening, I was bashing away on my laptop and all of a sudden I got this tingling feeling in my hands. This was more powerful than my 'tingles' though. This felt like there was electricity coming out of my fingers and my hands got really warm. I naturally have cold hands (don't they say that means I have a warm heart?), so just having warm hands in itself was quite a change to the norm.

My shoulder was tweaking a bit because I had been hunched over my laptop for a while (saying this has just made me sit up straight!) so I thought, "Give it a go Viv." I put my hand over my shoulder and left it there for a while. I immediately started feeling this warm 'liquid' running around my shoulder and within five minutes the pain had completely gone. Wow!

For the next few days I had a go at self-healing, by putting my hands over various points of my head and body and just leaving them there for a while.

Quite often when I had been doing meditations, I would get this sensation of purple liquid flooding into my head. When I had mentioned it at a meditation class, I was told that it is spiritual energy and a sign that I am really connected spiritually. Sometimes it is like a sort of cloudy lavender; sometimes it is like a purple liquid swirling around (a bit like when you see petrol on water) and other times it is like a 'lava lamp' where blobs of thicker purple liquid seem to drop into my head. There are times when it drops in so quickly that it fills my head with a 'sheet' of purple.

I have learned to understand that this is 'universal life force energy' and every time I did Reiki self-healing it absolutely flooded in. Within a few days I was feeling the most relaxed, calm and serene that I had done in a long time.

Every time I thought about Reiki I got the buzzing in my hands and Jean explained that just thinking the word 'Reiki' is what opens you up as a channel for it. It seemed to be flooding into me so I almost had to make a point of not thinking about it or purposefully 'switching it off'. My hands are buzzing a bit now just thinking about it.

I had only been 'attuned' for a few days but I was getting this overwhelming urge to perform Reiki healing on others. At the time, Jon was in absolute agony with one of his knees. It was so bad, he was limping quite badly and struggled to get up and down the stairs (poor old thing!).

I asked Jean if she thought it would be OK to perform some Reiki healing on Jon even though I had only been doing self-healing for a few days. She said "Viv, with you, we throw away the rule book. If it feels right just follow your intuition and do it."

So I did a Reiki healing session with Jon. I must admit, I was a little nervous, I wasn't sure if it was going to work and with Jon being very 'grounded' I thought I might make a bit of a fool of myself. But hey, I've been making a fool of myself in front of Jon for 25 years, and he's still hanging on in there, so what was any different?

I will let Jon tell you his 'grounded' view of the healing session in his View from the Ground section. I think it is much more powerful coming from a grounded person.

My friend Anj had been suffering really badly with labyrinthitis. We were out one day and she was talking about it. My hand started buzzing. I asked if I could put me hand near her ear (had to do it quite casually because we were out in public!). Anj describes the sensation as feeling like something was being pulled out of her ear – almost like a snake.

We resolved to do a proper Reiki session and a date was set. The connection between me and Anj was pretty powerful. It literally made my hair stand on end and afterwards we compared notes. The areas I had been guided to focus on (which happens when I get increased 'tingling' or purple energy flooding in) were places where Anj had had some previous issues and I was not aware of them. It was quite remarkable to know that I had been guided to just the right spots.

That night she texted me to say her ear had popped for the first time in months and the next day she felt better than she had done in ages. Magic!

I have performed Reiki on a number of people now and it just feels like such a blessing and a gift that I can help them. There is always a pretty powerful experience on both sides and a lot of healing going on.

My mum has suffered with rheumatoid arthritis for a number of years and it has the knock on effect of her suffering with things like sciatica and back pain. I gave her some Reiki the other night and also combined it with Ho'oponopono – powerful stuff! Mum said she was completely pain free for the whole session and at one point she felt like her body floated off the sofa and this 'rack' of pain just dropped away from her. She said it almost felt like a wooden rack.

So, I think you can see I am a firm advocate of Reiki. Not only does my daily self-healing keep me healthy in body and mind but I am also blessed to be able to channel this healing for others.

It is part of my daily life now and I have never felt better.

---

## View from the Ground

Now – Reiki?! At first, I have to admit to a raised eye brow or three (I am grounded but do have a third eye it would appear).

When Viv told me that Jean had carried out an attunement on her I was a bit baffled. This was something new to me and, as with all things new that I couldn't see, I found it hard to grasp.

However, as Viv has indicated, she performed two healing sessions for me. I had been suffering with an extremely painful right knee for the last three months, to the point where I was severely limping; couldn't run across a road, and thought I might need medical help. I don't do visiting the doctor, so the idea of going under the knife scared me. But being unable to walk scared me more.

Whilst I am not a natural athlete, I like running around on the beach when we're on holiday and chasing a rugby ball. So, I entrusted Viv's Reiki skills – two 45 minute sessions. During the 'experience' I felt a real sense of peace and tranquillity. However, one of the incredible things I remember was when Viv touched my forehead. Whilst her hands were warm, her finger tips were literally ice cold. Another memory of the second session, was it feeling like sparks were coming from Viv's hands. It may feel like I protest too much - I am a very grounded person but I genuinely had these feelings during the Reiki and it only adds to what, ultimately, was an amazing experience.

---

At first, I felt some easing of the pain but not the hoped for scream of, "I have no pain!" However, over the following days, the pain genuinely started to disappear, to the point where two weeks later, the pain had completely gone.

We're now four months on from my Reiki and I have no pain in my right knee, and I have not suffered my usual winter discomfort borne out of a fall many years ago, which historically has caused pain every winter just before it was due to snow. That's weird in itself.

**Jon**

## Connecting with Nature

*"One touch of nature makes the whole world kin."*
*WILLIAM SHAKESPEARE*

*"Look deep into nature and then you will understand everything better."*
*ALBERT EINSTEIN*

At the beginning of this book I was ever so slightly derisory towards 'hippy tree huggers'. I apologised at the time and said I thought you had got it right.

I know even more so now that you have got it right, although I haven't actually hugged any trees yet.

When I was thinking about this section, a memory came to mind. It was of a time when I was completely stressed out. It was at the peak of my challenging times when I did wonder how I was going to get through things.

I remember driving out to Malham Cove (a stunning area of the Yorkshire Dales) with Jon, Ben and Livia. I was in the passenger seat feeling (and trying to hide) completely stressed. Jon and the kids were laughing and joking, the music was playing and outwardly it was a very happy scene. Inwardly, I was in utter turmoil and felt completely disconnected from what was going on around me.

Now, I am no psychologist but I am sure when a person feels like they are completely disconnected from the realities of the world that they are near to tipping over the edge and that is exactly how I felt.

I held it together. You have to do when you're a mum. We arrived at Malham Cove, got our walking boots on and off we set. Within minutes, I begin to feel connected again and that I was back in my body.

The combination of vigorous walking (up a pretty steep hill) and the fresh air and beautiful scenery around me just completely brought me back down to earth (but in a nice way). I couldn't believe the contrast of how I had felt in the car and how I was feeling now, walking with my family in this beautiful countryside.

I have always loved walking and being outdoors. If it's out in the Yorkshire Dales, that is even better. But I had never quite appreciated the immense healing power of nature.

If you want to call me a 'hippy tree hugger' – hey, I embrace that completely and fully. You can never underestimate just how important nature is to us.

I realised that in connecting to nature in its purest form, it somehow connected me back into my body and more importantly, my mind.

It opened my eyes up to the beauty all around me and the abundance of nature. I know I might sound like I am going off on one a bit here, but it has been such an important part of my healing and dealing with day to day challenges that it deserves a place in this book.

I go out for a walk every day. I am lucky enough to live in a pretty nice area in Leeds on the border of the countryside, but quite often I just walk around the streets to get some fresh air.

When I walk around, I make a point of being in the 'here and now'. Thoughts crop up in my head but I quickly dismiss them and focus on what is around me. If I do think about anything, it is all the things I am grateful for and walking is a good time for me to combine being connected to nature with my thoughts of gratitude and a bit of Ho'oponopono thrown in.

I always feel completely invigorated when I get home.

So how do I manage to focus on all the nature around me and block out any negative thoughts. I focus on using all five senses as I walk around. What can I see? And then I see the plants or birds or friendly people walking past. What can I hear? Have you ever stopped outside and actually listened to the sounds around you. In the main I hear bird song and that is just so beautiful. What can I feel? I can feel the warmth of the sun on my back or the wind and rain on my face (more of the sun and less of the wind and rain would be good!). What can I touch? Don't do this one too often but just feeling my scarf wrapped around me or my feet in my walking shoes. What can I smell? The smell of blossom as you walk past; the smell of fresh cut grass (one of my favourites) or just smelling the fresh air and feeling it going up your nose. What can I taste? Well this is where I promise you I don't get down and start eating grass but even just feeling the air going into your mouth is a great feeling.

Right, I'll come back down from my 'at one with nature' lecture but I hope you can see just how much this has helped me.

When you are feeling stressed out and the world is getting on top of you – believe me the best thing to do is get yourself wrapped up (if you live in Leeds) and get out there for a power walk and some fresh air.

## View from the Ground

Strangely, I remember that drive to Malham Cove and kind of feel guilty. As a driver I used to be a bit high on emotion. Some people call this road rage. I just view it as recognising the incompetence of other drivers. However, due to an altercation with an average speed check camera on a local motorway, I was required to attend a speed awareness workshop. That, a bit like this book, was life changing and made me realise that I needed to slow down in every sense of the words.

As a result, I have become a more relaxed driver and I do remember that drive to Malham Cove and having a laugh with Ben and Liv, and taking in the magnificent scenery around us. What I missed was the turmoil that was being suffered in the seat next to me.

However, what I also remember - you can't forget it once you've been - is the beauty of the scenery and the effect that has on your attitude. It is also the effect of the fresh air that blasts you on the walks; the effects of eating lunch in God's dining room; and partaking a swift drink of rosé, which has somehow been packed with the picnic.

Nature is magic and one of the kicks up the backside you need when you're feeling a bit down or stressed.

As Viv says, we are lucky to live where we do. This gives us great opportunities to experience the great outdoors. But I strongly urge anyone and everyone who has been blessed with the ability to move to do so and experience the beauty of what we have around us.

If you can see it, be grateful and cherish what you can see; if you can hear it, celebrate and listen to the birds in the trees and the wind whistling around; if you can smell it, intake the incredible smells around us; if you can touch it, feel nature run between your fingers; and if you can taste it ................... be careful there are some poisonous berries out there.

Feel nature and celebrate!!!

**Jon**

# CHAPTER 7

## Fly Tunes

"Music has healing power. It has the ability to take
people out of themselves for a few hours."
ELTON JOHN

"For me, singing sad songs has a way of healing a situation.
It gets the hurt out in the open, into the light,
out of the darkness."
REBA McENTIRE

"I think music in itself is healing. It's an expression of humanity.
It's something we are all touched by. No matter what
culture we are from, everyone loves music."
BILLY JOEL

This is another Chapter that was not in my original plan for my book. As with a lot of things recently I had a little seed of an idea that grew in my mind with lots of little jigsaw pieces dropping in and then a flash of inspiration.

The first seed of the idea was the fact that as I have been writing this book, I always have music playing. Jon has done me a couple of playlists that have all the songs that have meant something to me during the turbulent times I have been going through. These are songs that either resonate with me because of the lyrics, or I quite simply just like the tune to dance around to and get my energy levels up.

I also strongly believe that a lot of answers from the higher realms come to us in music and I have had some quite astonishing experiences where I have been thinking about something or mulling over an issue and the answer has come to me in the next song that plays on the radio.

Writing the last chapter about connecting with nature and how therapeutic I find the sound of bird song was the last piece of the jigsaw and then everything else just dropped into place.

I have taken to putting my playlist on 'shuffle' when I start playing it and the first song always seems so relevant to my current situation at that particular time.

So where did the name for this chapter come from? Well it was another flash of inspiration. I was thinking about this new chapter and trying to work out the title. What title could I have that would link music to flying? I had been mulling over it for ages and couldn't think of one. Then in another flash of inspiration the words literally just popped into my head.

I immediately texted Jon feeling very clever (although I cannot lay claim to this idea being completely mine – I do feel it came from a higher source). He came back to say, "That's really good. It took me a bit to get it but genius!" It made me realise I'd better explain it. If you've already got it, fantastic, but for those who think a bit more on a logical basis here's the thinking. My playlist is on Jon's IPod. When I was mulling over the title, for some reason the word 'I-tunes' came into my head and then of course this immediately led to Fly Tunes!

I used three quotes in this section, mainly because I couldn't decide which one to drop. They summed up the healing power of music so well. Music is incredibly powerful and healing.

It has helped me to bring out all my hurt into the light and out of the darkness.

It has helped me to heal the hurt.

It has helped me to explosively express my humanity (I have sung some of these songs very angrily!).

It has helped me to release my inner child and dance like no one is watching me.

It has made me laugh and cry in equal measures and release all that emotion.

It has been the inspiration and 'light bulb' moment that represented my 'life purpose' and gave me the name for my new business, which has gathered some wonderful people around me.

And, most importantly it was the inspiration for the title of this book.

Music is a pretty personal thing in terms of what we like and don't like and what really resonates with each of us, but something has told me to put my playlist in this book with the specific lyrics that have helped me. They gave me a lot of guiding messages and really helped me so I share them with you in the hope that they help you too.

I also realised recently that it is different songs that now resonate with me (from the ones that resonated when I first started on this journey) and that if I put the playlist in a chronological order it represents my journey through song.

It has made me realise just how much I have come along since the start of my journey in discovering the power of my mind, and I thought that was quite a powerful message.

To explain how I have set this section out in the hope that you will get the most out of it. I have put the music into the three key stages of my journey.

The first stage was when I was feeling a little hopeless and scared and also a bit confused by the spiritual experiences I had been having. I was also grieving for my dad and trying to deal with the X Man at his worst.

Stage 2 is when I had realised there was only one person who could sort me out and that was ME. During this stage, I was still pretty stressed out by everything, but I was learning some new tools which were helping me to deal with it and I was beginning to realise the power of my mind.

Stage 3 is now.

For each song I have named the song and the artist plus the lyrics that really resonated with me.

Jon and I love watching Keith Lemon on TV in his programme 'Celebrity Juice'. He has a feature where if he has a musician in he holds up their CD and asks "What's the Message?". It's a bit difficult to capture how funny this is in print, but the title of the CD normally has a really obvious message and it is just very funny watching the artist trying to seriously explain the message. Jon and I have used this phrase quite a bit in a jokey way about various things in life so I felt like I should include this in my playlist. It is actually quite an important point. I have learned to look for the message in most things that come my way and have learned a lot about myself and situations by practising this habit regularly.

So, I have also included "What's the message?" for each song. In some songs it is pretty obvious but I will explain how it particularly resonated with me, at that particular point in my journey and how it helped me.

### Angels – Robbie Williams
*"I sit and wait. Does an angel contemplate my fate.*
*And do they know, the places where we go*
*when we're grey and old. Cos I've been told*
*that salvation lets their wings unfold"*

Message for me: Well this seems like a fairly obvious message. I have included this track in all three sections because different lyrics have resonated with me on my journey. The interesting thing here is that Robbie has always claimed this song was about his mum. I do think he may have had an experience similar to mine. The other thing I find wonderful is that after some pretty dark days himself, this was the track that relaunched Robbie into solo superstardom. I can still remember the first time I heard it and being blown away by the song and that it was Robbie Williams singing it. I think there was some divine inspiration here.

### People Help The People – Birdy
*"God knows what is hiding in those weak and drunken*
*hearts. Guess he kissed the girls and made them cry.*
*Those hard faced queens of misadventure.*
*God knows what is hiding in those weak and sunken lives.*
*Fiery thrones of muted angels, giving love and getting*
*nothing back. Oh…people help the people."*

Message for me: This song made me think of the X Man and me and represented my feelings around how I felt he was treating me. I had had my 'spiritual experience' at this point and learned about earth angels. This was also the absolute light bulb moment inspiration for the name of my new business.

## Help – Hurts
*"I'm sick and tired of being afraid. If I cry anymore then my tears will wash me away I can feel the darkness coming.......And I'm afraid of myself. Call my name and I'll come running. 'Cause I just need some help"*

Message for me: This was during a pretty dark time for me when I was feeling quite hopeless and didn't know where to turn for help.

## Shake It Out – Florence and the Machine
*"And every demon wants his pound of flesh.*
*But I like to keep some things to myself.*
*I like to keep my issues drawn. It's always darkest before the dawn…..And it's hard to dance with the devil on your back so shake him off."*

Message for me: This probably reflected some of my darker moments where I was thinking of the X Man as the devil and I really did want to shake him off. The phrase 'It's always darkest before the dawn' did give me some hope though! I also now realise that sometimes you have to experience a lot of darkness before you finally find your true self.

## Love Me Again – John Newman
*"Know I've done wrong, left your heart torn.*
*Is that what devils do? Took you so low, where only fools go.*
*I shook the angel in you! It's unforgivable. I stole and burnt your soul. Is that what demons do, hey? They rule the worst of me. Destroy everything.*
*They bring down angels like you!."*

Message for me: This was another rather indulgent song for me. Again I was seeing the X Man as the devil and me as an angel!

## Shine – Take That

*"You, you're such a big star to me. You're everything
I wanna be. But you're stuck in a hole and I want you
to get out. I don't know what there is to see,
but I know it's time for you to leave. We're all
just pushing along trying to figure it out..."*

Message for me: Interestingly, I think this is Mark Owen
singing to Robbie Williams in his darker days. Sorry if I
have got this wrong Mark! This resonated with me because
I realised I was stuck and I knew it was time for me to leave,
but I couldn't figure it out.

## Iridescent – Linkin Park

*"When you were standing in the wake of devastation.
When you were waiting on the edge of the unknown.
With the cataclysm raining down, your insides crying,
"Save me now" You were there, impossibly alone.......
Do you feel cold and lost in desperation? You build up hope,
but failures all you've known. Remember all the sadness
and frustration and let it go."*

Message for me: This was when I began to realise that I had
to let these negative thoughts go. I was spiralling downwards
through obsessing about my situation and this song made
me realise I had to let it go.

## Wake Me Up – Avicii

*"Feeling my way through the darkness, guided by a
beating heart. I can't tell where the journey will end,
but I know where to start......They say I'm caught up in a
dream....well life will pass be by if I don't open up my eyes.
Well that's fine by me....All this time I was finding myself
and I didn't know I was lost....I tried carrying the weight
of the world but I only had two hands."*

Message for me: At this point I was still feeling very sorry for
myself but I was realising that I had to follow my heart and

that was the best guide. By this time I also had realised what my life purpose was and this song helped me to understand to not worry about where things would end but to just get started. I did still feel like I was carrying the weight of the world on my shoulders!

## Viva La Vida – Cold Play

*"I used to roll the dice. Feel the fear in my enemy's eyes. Listen as the crowd would sing, "Now the old king is dead! Long live the king. One minute I held the key, next the walls were closed on me. And I discovered that my castle stands on pillars of salt and pillars of sand."*

Message for me: This track makes me think of the X Man. It has been a big learning for me to really analyse his behaviour and what it did to our business and for a long time I just sat there and allowed it to happen around me. This was the point when I began to realise that I could no longer be in an environment that completely went against my values.

## Don't You Worry Child – Swedish House Mafia

*"There was a time, I used to look into my father's eyes. In a happy home, I was a king I had a golden throne. Those days are gone, now the memory's on the wall……… Up on the hill across the blue lake, that's where I had my first heart break. I still remember how it all changed. My father said, "Don't you worry, don't you worry child. See heaven's got a plan for you."*

Message for me: This track helped me to realise that up until recently, I had led a pretty blessed life. It helped me to accept that to move forward and develop as a human being you do have to face challenges. That is how your soul grows. It also made me think of my dad and how he had told me that everything happens for a reason. This has given me a lot of comfort when I have been facing difficult situations and it has helped me to focus more on what life lesson I am learning – rather than feeling sorry for myself.

## Counting Stars – One Republic

*"Lately, I've been, I've been losing sleep. Dreaming about the things that we could be. But baby I been I been praying hard. Said no more counting dollars. We'll be counting stars....I feel the love and I feel it burn. Down this river, every turn. Hope is a four letter word. Take that money, watch it burn, sink in the river, the lessons are learned."*

Message for me: This was quite a profound one for me. Up until this point I had been focussing all my 'Law of Attraction' energies on money and it wasn't really working. I realised that I had to focus on good outcomes for me and others and that I was being a bit selfish. It also made me realise how I had spent so much time 'counting dollars' I had forgotten what is truly important in life and I was been given a tough lesson to realise this. My lesson was that you should focus on 'counting stars'. In other words, focus on what good you can do to perhaps bring a bit of light to the world and if you focus just on money then you will have to watch it burn to learn what is truly important in life.

## Angels – Robbie Williams

*" And down the waterfall, wherever it may take me,*
*I know that life won't break me when I come to call.*
*She won't forsake me. I'm lovin' angels instead.*
*When I'm feelin' weak and my pain walks down*
*a one way street, I look above and I know*
*I'll always be blessed with love."*

Message for me: As I moved into this next phase of my life, I was still a little battered and torn but I was beginning to realise there was more to this life than what we just see in front of us. I began to feel very protected and safe and this gave me the strength to carry on with what I knew was going to be an even greater turbulence of change. I knew it was going to get a little bit worse before it got better, but I also knew that it was well worth it.

## Tub Thumping – Chumbawamba

*"I get knocked down and I get up again. You're never*
*going to keep me down"*

*Message for me: My personal fight back was starting. I was not going to let this situation beat me!!!! I was bouncing back!*

## Heart of Courage – Two Steps To Hell
## Archangel – Two Steps to Hell

There are no lyrics to these tracks but they are awesome. If you want some music to just completely lose yourself in then this is it. It gives me goosebumps just thinking about the music. It is so rousing!

## Titanium – David Guetta

*You shout it out, but I can't hear a word you say.*
*I'm talking loud not saying much.*
*I'm criticized but all your bullets ricochet. You shoot me down, but I get up. I'm bulletproof, nothing to lose, fire away, fire away. Ricochet, you take your aim, fire away, fire away. Cut me down, but it's you who'll have further to fall.*
*Ghost town and haunted love.*
*Raise your voice, sticks and stones may break my bones. Stone-hard, machine gun*
*Firing at the ones who run. Stone-hard as bulletproof glass. You shoot me down but I won't fall I am titanium.*

Message for me: This was my anthem for a long time was regaining my confidence and self esteem. This was also the peak of some pretty horrendous times with the X Man and this song really gave me a lot of strength. I would put it on full blast in the house and sing it as loud as I could. This song taught me that it was down to me what impact another person could have on me and I was strong enough to defend myself against any 'bullets'! I guess you could call this my 'angry' phase. I think when you are going through turbulence you have to go through an 'angry' phase. It is almost a release of all that pent up negative energy that has been building in your mind and body. This song certainly helped me to release a lot of it. For me it was the turning point from being a victim to taking responsibility for how I was feeling.

## Roar – Katy Perry

*"I used to bite my tongue and hold my breath,*
*scared to rock the boat and make a mess. So I sat quietly, agreed politely. I guess that I forgot I had a choice.*

*I let you push me past the breaking point.*
*I stood for nothing, so I fell for everything.*
*You held me down, but I got up, already brushing*
*off the dust. You hear my voice, your hear that sound,*
*like thunder, gonna shake the ground. You held*
*me down, but I got up. Get ready 'cause*
*I had enough. I see it all, I see it now.*
*I got the eye of the tiger, a fighter,*
*dancing through the fire. 'Cause I am a champion,*
*and you're gonna hear me roar.*
*Now I'm floating like a butterfly, stinging like*
*a bee I earned my stripes. I went from zero,*
*to my own hero"*

Message for me: This song was just absolutely perfectly timed. I was still slightly in my 'angry' phase but I had also done a lot of self-development by this point and I was becoming stronger and stronger. I was getting quite proud of myself and by this time some of the wonderful 'flock' had gathered around me and I was feeling much stronger because of their love and support. I had literally gone from zero to being my own hero. The key thing this song gave me was that I had not been standing in my own truth for many years. I had allowed someone to scare me so much that I was not standing up for my own values and what I believed in. This was when I began to truly learn some very important life lessons.

## Shine – Take That
*"I don't know what there is to see, but I know it's time*
*for you to leave. We're all just pushing along trying to figure*
*it out, out, out. All your anticipation pulls you down when*
*you can have it all. So come on, get it on*
*I don't know what you're waiting for. Your time is coming*
*don't be late, So come on, see the light on your face.*
*Let it shine, just let it shine, let it shine.*

*Stop being so hard on yourself. It's not good for your
health. I know that you can change. So clear your head
and come 'round. You only have to open your eyes,
you might just get a big surprise. And it may feel good
And you might want to smile, smile, smile.
Oh don't you let your demons pull you down.
'Cause you can have it all."*

Message for me: I realised I needed to stop dithering and do what I knew was the right thing to do. I needed to stop mulling over things and beating myself up over what had happened in the past. At this point I had started writing this book and the words in Shine just really resonated with me.

## What Doesn't Kill You Makes
## You Stronger – Kelly Clarkson

*"You know the bed feels warmer sleeping here alone.
You know I dream in colour and do the things I want.
You think you got the best of me. Think you've had the
last laugh. Bet you think that everything good is gone.
Think you left me broken down. Think that I'd come running
back. Baby you don't know me, cause you're dead wrong.
What doesn't kill you makes you stronger. Stand a little
taller. Doesn't mean I'm lonely when I'm alone.
What doesn't kill you makes a fighter,
footsteps even lighter."*

The message for me: This is just a real power song. It pretty much says it all for how I was feeling when I had made the decision that I didn't need the X Man and I could do this on my own. It also reminded me of just how strong I was and I began to rebuild my self-esteem and feel quite proud of myself. It also reminded me that the most important thing was to be happy and even if this meant putting myself into slightly scary territory on my own that this was preferable to staying with someone who made me unhappy.

## Hall of Fame – The Script

*"Don't wait for luck. Dedicate yourself and you could find yourself. You can go the distance, you can run the mile. You can walk straight through hell with a smile. You can be the hero, you can get the gold. Breaking all the records they thought never could be broke. Do it for your people. Do it for your pride. Never gonna know if you never even try. Do it for your country. Do it for your name. Cause there's gonna be a day standing in the hall of fame. And the world's gonna know your name. Cause you burn with the brightest flame."*

Message for me: This just became my anthem for the future. It made me realise that you can really do anything if you put your mind to it. If you follow your dream with determination and passion and a real belief in yourself you can do almost anything – including being famous. It gave me a real boost for my book and I began to think. This really could be a success. Other people around me were reading the book and saying how powerful it was. I started to dream about being a best-selling author and spreading my story out to the widest possible audience in the hope it would help others - that spurred me on.

## Stage 3 – These Wings Transform

So this is where I am right now and I truly do know that I have transformed.

These are songs that I just love dancing around to and it is so wonderful to look back over the story of my journey in music and see where I am now after a relatively short space of time.

I'm not going to put a 'message under each of these because there is just one overall message. I am happy. I am confident. I am fulfilled. I feel brave and strong. These lyrics all reflect how I am feeling right now and the songs will always be guaranteed to make me 'sing like no one is listening' and 'dance like no one is watching'!

### Angels – Robbie Williams
*"And through it all she offers me protection,*
*a lot of love and affection. Whether I'm right or wrong."*

### Love Me Again – John Newman
*"Here with all the strength I've found,*
*there's nothing I can't do."*

### Wake Me Up – Avicii
*"Life's a game made for everyone and love is the prize."*

### Diamonds – Rihanna
*"Find light in the beautiful sea. I choose to be happy.*
*You and I, we're like diamonds in the sky.*
*You're a shooting star I see, a vision of ecstasy.*

*So shine bright tonight, you and I, we're beautiful like*
*diamonds in the sky. Eye to eye, so alive.*
*We're beautiful like diamonds in the sky."*

Just interrupting to put a very small message in here.
Diamonds have come to be very significant in my life
because they come up a lot in my Shamanic Meditations
and they represent me. The first Shamanic Mediation I ever
did included a diamond and it was in this meditation that
I was told that writing a book was my future. That was what
got me fired to start writing. Jon will tell you an amazing story
about 'messages from on high' here. It needs to be in his
'grounded' bit as it was a little off the scale.

## One Day Like This – Elbow
*"Drinking in the morning sun. Blinking in the morning sun.*
*Shaking off the heavy one. Heavy like a loaded gun."*

## Feeling Good – Nina Simone
*"Birds flying high you know how I feel. Sun in the sky you*
*know how I feel. Breeze driftin' on by you know how I feel.*
*It's a new dawn. It's a new day. It's a new life for me.*
*And I'm feeling good, yeah."*

## On Top of The World – Imagine Dragons
*"I've had the highest mountains; I've had the deepest*
*rivers. You can have it all but life keeps moving. I take it in*
*but don't look down...Been waiting on this for a while now.*
*Paying my dues to the dirt. I've been waiting to smile.*
*Been holding it in for a while. Take you with me if I can.*
*Been dreaming of this since a child....I've tried to cut these*
*corners. Try to take the easy way out. I kept on falling*
*short of something. I could a gave up then but then again*
*I couldn't have cause I've travelled all this way for*
*something. I take it in but don't look down.*
*'Cause I'm on top of the world!"*

## Burn – Ellie Goulding

*We, we don't have to worry about nothing. Cause we got the fire and we're burning one hell of a something. They gonna see us from outer space...Light it up, like we're the stars of the human race. We'll be raising our hands, shining up to the sky, cause we got the fire, fire, fire. And we gonna let it burn burn burn burn*

## Wings – Birdy

*"Sunlight comes creeping in illuminates our skin. We watched the day go by. Stories of what we did. It made me think of you. Under a trillion stars, we danced on top of cars.... Oh lights go down. In the moment we're lost and found. If these wings could fly - For the rest of our lives."*

Sorry. I know I said I wasn't going to comment after these tracks and I've already done it once!! But this one is an important story of synchronicity. I had reached a point where I knew I was going to write a book. I was actually writing it, but the one thing I didn't have was a title. I'd toyed with a few ideas. I wanted something that represented angels, because this was how my whole experience had started, but I didn't want it to be too obvious. I also wanted it to be a title that suggested soaring and freedom. I had been struggling a bit and then Jon bought me the latest Birdy CD. I sat listening to it one day as I was typing my book. The rest as they say is history. Even more profound given another Birdy song gave me the name for my new business and future. I really do hope I get to meet Birdy and thank her one day.

## View from the Ground

My first thought is, what a great various artists CD that Viv has just put out there for some wise music label to do a compilation (I was going to say record label but that sounds old).

Music has formed an important part of my own life and a very important part of my life with Viv – and Ben & Liv. I use it at every given opportunity, be it in the car; in the dining room; on the train to and from London; on the beach; whenever. I am lucky enough to go to concerts and festivals with varying combinations of Viv, Ben, and / or Liv.

One concert that will always stick in my mind is when we saw Imagine Dragons last year. It had been a particularly horrendous day courtesy of the X Man. Viv and I really were not in the mood to stand with 2,000 others. We arrived at the venue and Viv wanted a glass of wine. I couldn't have one because I was driving, so had a huff. Liv wanted to stand somewhere near the bar because it was a good view, I didn't want to stand there because people with drinks would knock into me.

The downward spiral was there waiting, and I was ready to jump on it. Then, the band hit the stage and BANG!!!! The magic took over, it was as if the band were playing exclusively for the four of us. We spent the next 90 minutes singing, waving our arms, hugging, and just being daft. Pure, total magic and it took away all of the pain of the day. Thank you to a magnificent band.

As Viv has said, I have put together playlists for her, which have been great for Viv when working on this book. I would have to say, being accosted by Katie Perry roaring when I walk through the door after a long day in the office, or having Ellie Goulding burn me, can sometimes be pushing the boundaries!

We had one of those funny' coincidences' the other day (I know, I should call it synchronicity!). Viv had just done her first Shamanic Meditation and had been given various messages. You'll see the full story in her next book but the key messages were that she would be writing a book and she was represented as a diamond. We were talking about the meditation in the car and how interesting it was that the X Man called her a diamond when he first met her. Viv said, "Right let's see if there is a message about me writing a book, in the next song that plays on the radio." What came on next?

"Diamonds" by Rihanna. I nearly crashed the car!!! I think that was a strong message!

However, to see the effect these songs and others have had in Viv rediscovering her true self - her diamond - have been a joy to behold. So, a heartfelt thank you to the performers, and the lyricists who have had such a remarkable influence on her and on us. I am confident, through this book, we will be blessed with the opportunity to meet you and thank you personally.

Just to finish here, I would like to quote the lyrics from one song that means a lot to us both.

You're The Inspiration – Chicago.

"You're the meaning in my life. You're the inspiration. You bring feeling to my life. You're the inspiration"

It meant a lot as we took our first formal dance on 02 September 1989 (our wedding day).

It means more now. With all my heart, thank you.

**Jon**

# CHAPTER 8

## These Wings Can Fly!

*"Jump and you will find out how to unfold your wings as you fall."*
*RAY BRADBURY*

*"Love and desire are the spirit's wings to great deeds."*
*JOHANN WOLFGANG VON GOETHE*

*"Isn't it strange that princes and kings*
*And clowns that juggle in circus rings*
*And ordinary people, like you and like me*
*Are keepers of eternity?*
*To each is given a set of tools,*
*An hourglass and a book of rules*
*And each must build ere his time is done*
*A stumbling block or a stepping stone."*
*UNKNOWN*

Well, I can't quite believe we are nearing the end of this book. I hope I now hear a collective groan because you have all enjoyed it so much and don't want the book to finish!

For this Chapter I am back in the here and now and it is quite dramatic because I am currently going through the final 'extraction' and 'freedom' process and it is proving somewhat turbulent.

I look back over the last few months and think. Wow! If I had been dealing with what I am dealing with right now as the person of eighteen months ago I don't think I would have made it.

It has made me realise just how much I have developed. It has also made me realise the absolute awesome power of our minds. The way I look at things now is just poles apart from how I used to look at things.

I come at everything now from a calm and thoughtful approach. Nothing really flusters me anymore. I can be completely in the here and now and feel very grounded (honest!) but with a strong protection around me and I have realised this is down to the strengthening of my mind. The protection I have around me is ME!

I also have the love and protection of all those around me and that is a force to be reckoned with.

I want to share with you some quite amazing experiences I have had over the last few days which I absolutely believe have been timed to coincide with me nearly finishing this book. This is synchronicity at its best and the 'spiritual' side of things at its most magical.

The last few days have propelled me to take that final 'leap of faith' and as Ray Bradbury says, my wings did unfold and quite amazingly.

## *Divine Intervention*

*"I'd learned enough from life's experiences to understand that
destiny's interventions can sometimes be read as invitation
for us to address and even surmount our biggest fears.
It doesn't take a great genius to recognize that when
you are pushed by circumstance to do the one thing you
have always most specifically loathed and feared, this can be,
at the very least, an interesting growth opportunity."*
ELIZABETH GILBERT

*"Why do we mortals wonder if it is through 'human chaos' or
through 'divine perfection' when the world guides us to some
magical event? In either case, is not the result the same?
Is the result not 'divine perfection?*
ROMAN PAYNE

What I am about to tell you – you just could not make up. But it is all true and I have my 'grounded' Jon to verify.

For some time, I have been getting more and more pressing 'thoughts' about leaving the X Man. This is very difficult when you are tied financially into a business and is what has held me back for a long time.

There have been a number of things I have seen and read recently which were all saying the same thing. I have learned to take note of things when I get increasing repeat messages from various sources, but for some reason I was doggedly ignoring them. In fact I know why I was doggedly ignoring them. I was scared! I knew this was going to be the final leap of faith and it was frightening me a little.

But the messages kept coming. They came more often, from all sorts of angles and were getting increasingly clear.

I now realise that you cannot move on with your life unless you get rid of some things that are holding you back or filling your space. You basically have to have a good clear out and create some space.

When you create space in your life, you create a vacuum and the Universe has to fill it. If there is something in your life that is not serving you or your life purpose then it will always hold you back until you release it. I could not get this idea of creating a 'vacuum' out of my head and I knew it was an important message for me.

So, I resolved to have a good clear out. I read something about 'giving up' material things that you no longer need. How many times have I walked to my wardrobe, looked in and seen it crammed with clothes and yet there is just a tiny proportion of these that I wear. The message given was that if you are hanging onto things (just in case!) this is like carrying psychic energy and it carries with it a story of lack and fear. Make room for new things and get that psychic energy circulating!! When I first read this I was less than convinced!

Then I really thought about it and realised it was correct. Why was I hanging on to all these things if I never wore them? It was actually pretty greedy and selfish because someone else could be benefiting from my clothes and there they were gathering dust in my wardrobe. So one afternoon, Jon and I had a fabulous time just throwing clothes into black bin bags to go to the charity shop. It felt great, very cleansing and we also had a bit of a laugh looking at all the old clothes we had hung onto. Can you believe, Jon found a bright yellow polka dot tie! When did he ever wear that? It also felt great because we knew others would be able to use the clothes. 'What's one man's junk is another man's treasure.'

I had also been giving my subconscious mind a good clear out with the releasing and forgiving exercises I mentioned in the previous chapter.

But there was still one big elephant in the room and that was the X Man.

I could not ignore these messages any more, but I was ignoring them and I was almost burying my head in the sand and hoping it would all go away.

Then something happened last weekend which was so amazing it just could not be ignored.

Last Sunday I was doing my usual morning 'ablutions' getting ready in the bathroom. I pottered into the bedroom and something caught my eye. There was movement to my left.

I have a plaque attached to the wall which has all hooks on it. It is designed to hang jewellery from and I have all my necklaces hanging from it. I also have my crystal (I've mentioned this before in the section on chakras and seeing their energy) hanging on one of these hooks.

As I looked towards where the movement had caught my eye, I was rather blown away to see the crystal moving. A very regular backward and forward swinging movement. Bearing in mind this was against a wall and none of the necklaces were moving, it was quite a phenomenon to see. I even called Jon to come and look at it because I couldn't believe what I was seeing.

I need to take just one step back here as I don't think I have mentioned this. When Kathy first gave me the crystal pendant, she said, "You can ask it questions you know." I was like, "What??!!!!" Anyway, me being me, I decided to give it a go. You basically ask Yes and No type questions. You can test how the crystal will answer you by asking questions you know have 'yes and no' answers to them.

I always start with, "Is my name Vivienne?" and get a very definite backwards and forwards swing. I then say "Is my name Jon?" and it stays completely still. So I know how my crystal works but I still do this little check at the beginning of any question and answers session.

So I did the above. Then I said, "Is there something you need to tell me?" the crystal swung pretty strongly to say

'Yes'. In fact it almost hit me in the face I had it so close to me and it swung so strongly! I then said, "Is it about the X Man?" (I did use his proper name at this point by the way). The crystal swung again.

Now, I realised I had a bit of a dilemma here. I had never had this type of 'conversation' with my crystal before. How was I going to think of the right question for it to answer 'Yes' or 'No' to. I could be there all day!

Then I had a 'light bulb' moment. I said, "Shall I do a Shamanic Meditation so you can give me the message there?" I was nearly knocked out again!!

So, having narrowly avoided a couple of black eyes, I went downstairs to get myself set up for a Shamanic Meditation.

Here's how it went.

---

### Knowing What the Crystal wanted me to know - 02 March 2014

I was at the top of a hill sitting under a tree. I lay down and looked up through the leaves. There were wind chimes and I could hear them and the leaves rustling in the breeze. I was dressed in traditional Red Indian warrior type clothing

An angel appeared and held out its hand. I took its hand and started walking with it. I sprouted wings.

We walked towards some golden gates and walked through them. There was all swirly white mist – like clouds. I walked through the white swirly mist for a while and then it went really dark.

I couldn't see anything (it felt like I was in the night sky) but I could see a light ahead of me so I aimed for that. When I got to the light it was like a spinning vortex and I knew I had to go into it.

I heard the words 'go with the flow'. I just got in and let it carry me along.

I plopped out of the vortex, rather unceremoniously, into what looked like an old dusty chapel. It was all brown and grey and gloomy. There were some people sitting on pews to my right and they all looked really downtrodden and sad and poorly. They were all in brown clothes. The Big Indian Chief was stood opposite them watching them and me.

I held my hands out towards them and this green mist came out. It started spreading over them and covering them. Gradually everyone started to brighten up and look happier and healthier and the scene became really colourful. They were all healed and I heard the words, "Spread your love."

The Chief led me out of another door and I was in a forest. The people followed behind me all smiling and happy. Ahead of me on the horizon was a huge sunset. I walked towards the sunset.

As I got nearer, an elephant walked across the sunset silhouetted and it was carrying what looked like a royal box on top of it.

When I reached the sunset, I could feel its heat but I walked right through it.

When I came out of the other side I was dressed in different clothes. What I would call Red Indian finery but still kind of 'warrior' type dress. I heard the words "You have been transformed."

The Big Indian Chief and Angel had reappeared and they handed me a golden sword and a golden shield. They said to me, "You must fight for these people."

We were in quite a barren rocky type environment and there was a rocky hill ahead of us. We started walking towards it. The Indian Chief and Angel were really close at my side and just slightly behind me, so I was leading the way.

As we reached the rocky hill I noticed a dragon curled up and sleeping in the entrance to a cave. I stopped in my tracks and heard the words, "You must slay the dragon."

I was really hesitant and started walking towards the dragon but kept stopping and looking behind me to make sure the Indian Chief and Angel were still there and they were. I did dither about a bit but kept moving forward with trepidation. The dragon stirred and got up.

It let out an almighty roar and breathed fire all over me. I heard, "You will be OK, we are protecting you." The amazing thing was that although I could feel heat and it literally blew my hair off my face (it felt like a really strong hurricane!) – it didn't burn me. It just felt like hot air. The Angel and Indian Chief sprinkled some golden dust on me and it put a white light around me.

This repeated a few times as I got nearer and nearer to the dragon (it breathing fire at me and it not burning me and me being sprinkled with gold dust) and although I was confident it couldn't burn me I was still dragging my feet a bit!!! I really did not want to go near it. The word 'dithering' popped into my head.

When I got really close I could see that the dragon was shackled and chained to the cave. I heard, "He is chained to his cave. You have to get the diamond."

There was a diamond on a plinth next to him and I could see he was guarding it. I dithered about again moving closer and closer to him and then I heard, "You have to get the diamond!" and it spurred me on.

I started running really fast towards the dragon. It let out an almighty roar and breathed fire on me and I held up my shield which protected me. Every time the dragon roared, rocks and stones started falling above it from the rock face but it seemed oblivious to them and just kept roaring.

I got to the plinth and grabbed the diamond – the dragon came at me and I lashed out with my sword which wounded him slightly, but he carried on roaring and breathing fire on me.

More and more rocks were starting to fall and I knew I had to get away from there fast. I ran away and when I turned around the dragon had been buried by all the rocks and stones he had caused to fall.

I ran back to the Chief and Angel and put the diamond to my chest. It started to open up and all green mist came out. It started spreading further and further out from the diamond and then it was coming out of my chest and my hands.

It carried on spreading and spreading across the land. The people that were enveloped in it all turned from grey, brown and sad to happy and carefree and dressed in white.

Loads of plants and flowers started sprouting up and wherever the green mist went there was complete abundance.

I got back to the tree and looked back on all the happy people and abundance before me.

Well... I think that was someone trying to give me a very strong message.

There are a number of really key things here.

The diamond has appeared in a lot of my Shamanic Meditations. I looked back over the documents I have put together with all my meditations and the very first one I ever did had a diamond in it. When I asked what the diamond represented, I was told, "It represents You." This had reminded me that when I first met the X Man there was something he said which was a bit unusual. He said to Jon, "Viv is a diamond and there aren't many like her." It had made me feel quite good at the time, but little did I know that four years later it would feature so much as a representation of me.

So, I was effectively getting myself back. I had interpreted it as getting my heart back and Jean interpreted it as getting my 'energy' back from the X Man. Well here I was being told it was actually about getting ME back.

I think we all know who the dragon is. He is 'shackled to his cave' by his own previous actions and behaviour and I think this was another very powerful message.

He also breathes a heck of a lot of 'hot air' – which in the past has really frightened me and I now realise that I have a protective shield from it and that there are others right behind me and alongside me who will protect me.

I also realised, that I had been dithering for way too long. I honestly really did dither in this Shamanic Meditation and it actually looked quite comical at the time, but the words 'stop dithering!' kept going through my head.

# The Final Release

"The release of atomic energy has not created a new problem.
It has merely made more urgent the necessity
of solving an existing one."
ALBERT EINSTEIN

"It takes a lot of courage to release the familiar and seemingly
secure to embrace the new. But there is no real security
in what is no longer meaningful. There is more security in
the adventurous and exciting for in movement there is life
and in change there is power."
ALAN COHEN

The Shamanic Meditation gave me the confidence and the impetus to do what I should have done a very long time ago. If only I had stopped dithering!

That evening, I was going through a workbook that Jean had given me, Anj and Bernie for us to complete in time for our next team meeting. It was a business type workbook, designed to help you put the words together for an 'elevator pitch' about your business, as we were trying to get this finalised for People Help People.

It was one of these workbooks where you get some words in a sentence with some 'blanks' that you have to fill in with your own words. I decided I wasn't going to think too hard about it, 'go with the flow' and just see what words came out.

I was quite surprised at what came out because, and it is only today that I realise, it actually gave me the 'script' for my forthcoming discussion with the X Man.

At the time, I didn't think this, but looking back I now see that this was almost my workbook from the Universe to prepare me for the conversation I was about to have with the X Man and to give me the words that I needed to say to him. Now that's what I call synchronicity! Thanks Jean.

So here are the words that I came up with in going through this exercise:

> One of the most important high impact experiences of my life was when I had to deal with a very challenging person for a sustained period of time.
>
> The most important thing I learned from that experience is to stand in my own truth, to follow my heart and to stand by my values.
>
> Now I bring that learning to other people by sharing my experiences and how I overcame the challenges and hopefully, helping others to see that you can rise above turbulence in your life.
>
> The most important influences on the way that I am are my own values and a strong desire to give people the best possible support.
>
> Now that I have studied spiritual and scientific approaches to the power of the mind I have also taken this a step further in that I have written a book and I hope to inspire others with my story.

I was going to take that leap of faith and just follow my heart and retrieve 'myself' after four years of having being imprisoned and guarded by someone else.

I had been helped with the words I needed to say, so now it was just a matter of me building up the courage to say them.

And I did.

The X Man had sent me a text saying, "We really need to talk." And I replied to say, "Yes we really do."

The conversation started with the usual 'roaring' from the X Man. I let him say his piece and then I responded in a way he had never heard before and I think it completely threw him.

All the way through the conversation I maintained my composure, I responded rather than reacted and I told the X Man exactly what lessons I had learned.

The key was that I told him I had let my head rule for too long. I told him that my health and happiness were way more important than any money. I told him he had taken me to the abyss too many times – I had stared into it and been scared – but I realised now that jumping into the abyss was actually my preferred choice if it enabled me to release myself from him.

During our conversation I was very conscious of what I had learned about 'oneness and unity'. I wish the X Man no harm – quite the opposite, I sincerely want all that is good for him and his family. I focussed on how we could sort this situation out together so that we could both move on as quickly as possible with our own lives. It was going to be no use to either one of us if we continued at each others throats. I was also very conscious of the Shamanic Meditation and the analogy I had been given of the dragon roaring so loudly and persistently that he ended up burying himself under his own rocks. That is going to be up to the X Man, as to how much he roars now. All I know is that I got back to the safety of those who are protecting me, with my diamond intact.

I am also very grateful to him. I alluded to this at the beginning of my book and you are probably now wondering, "How the heck could Viv be grateful to the X Man?" Well, without him, I would not have travelled this journey and I would not have written this book. I would not have been forced to reflect on myself and my life and think about the lessons I had learned. I would probably have repeated my life pattern again with someone else and still be going round in circles in a lot of pain.

Without the X Man, I would not be where I am now - the happiest, healthiest and most fulfilled that I have been for many years.

I realise now I had to be absolutely 'jolted' and taken to the limits of my own humanity to begin to rebuild myself as the person I am really destined to be on this earth.

I now have such a sense of tranquillity and yet focus and purpose, that I do know that I have truly found my life's flight path.

I have had to go through quite a lot of turbulence to get there but I know now that it had to happen. I hope this gives you comfort if you are going through turbulence right now. It is for a reason. Try to look beyond the immediate stresses and think what this situation may be trying to tell you.

So, I had just created a BIG vacuum in my life. I now awaited with anticipation to see what would happen next and what would fill this vacuum.

*"Have the courage to say no. Have the courage to face the truth. Do the right thing because it is right. There are no magic keys to living your life with integrity."*
*W CLEMENT STONE*

*"Magic is believing in yourself. If you can do that, you can make anything happen."*
*JOHANN WOLFGANG VON GOETHE*

Anj had a dream. Here's what she said in an email to me:

> Last night I woke at 4:30. I asked my angels to help me get back to sleep and for me to wake up knowing what to do with xx's situation. Well...
>
> I dreamt that I was in a very big, white split level apartment which I shared with two others. Techy types, a man and a woman. Downstairs was a bit full of their techy stuff. They weren't very significant in this dream though. The upper level was a large room and there were about 20 people there, with a man who was some kind of clairvoyant sharing a piece of information with each of us. He got to me and said 'the light through the trees' but couldn't continue as a young Indian girl who was two places away from me interrupted him. I politely told her that he'd been giving me information and that I wanted to hear it. Although she continued to say something, he turned his attention back to me.

He opened up a brightly coloured book to a certain page and pointed to a stylised image of an orangey brown elephant. Underneath were written certain key words and numbers. I couldn't read all of them in time, but the first two numbers were 39 and 999. The book closed and when I reopened it to try find the description, I wasn't able to.

Here's what I found when I looked them up:

YOU ALREADY HAVE ALL THE TOOLS YOU NEED TO ACCOMPLISH WHAT YOU DESIRE. JUST GO FOR IT. -ELEPHANT

The colour maroon or a reddish-brown colour signifies dignity, nobility, power or it could represent a wealthy woman.

Elephant's medicine includes strength, royalty, connection to ancient wisdom, removal of obstacles and barriers, confidence, patience, using education opportunities, commitment, gentleness, communicating in relationships, discernment, intelligence, compassion. If this is your animal guide, these virtues are a part of your natural character. By applying them in your life, soul evolution is accomplished.

Number 39: Higher Powers sent you a message about your life path. Your natural abilities are very important for the place where you live and for all the people around you. Use them and Powers from above will help you with anything you need. Ask for guidance in your meditation or prayers if you have any doubts about yourself. It also means 12 (3+9) which is a message to have faith that the Spirit is supporting you.

Number 999: Get to work, Lightworker! The world needs your Divine life purpose right now. Fully embark upon your sacred mission without delay or hesitation.

Now, this just blew both of us away. It was almost like my Shamanic Meditation and Anj's dream had somehow crossed over. Anj is supporting someone who is going through a really challenging time at the moment and had asked for some answers.

The fact that I had seen a random elephant in my meditation (with a royal box on top of it) and didn't really understand the significance was suddenly made clear to me. The even more astonishing fact was that the elephant Anj had seen was orangey brown and I had seen my elephant going across an orangey brown sunset just. This just blew me away.

Anj and I are pretty connected but I hadn't realised we were THIS connected. It kind of took it to a whole new level and it felt there were messages for both of us in the dream and the meditation.

The next morning Anj was tidying up outside and found a little wooden cornflower blue butterfly.

Cornflower blue butterflies feature a lot in my meditations and I think they represent this book, it's front cover and colour theme.

That evening, I got a call from a friend, who had been going through a bit of turmoil at work caused by one particular person. Her bosses hadn't done anything about it and she had had no choice but to look for another job. I had been helping her to overcome feelings of guilt about looking for another job and she had recently gone for an interview. She rang me to let me know she had got the job!

While I was chatting to her, I spotted an email from a publisher in my inbox. I wanted to focus on my friend so moved away from my laptop. After we had finished talking I walked to my laptop closed my eyes and opened the email.

The publishers had seen the first three chapters of this book and now wanted to see the rest of it. The vacuum I had created was beginning to fill.

## Graduation from Flying School

*"We are taught, you must blame your father, your sisters, your brothers, the school, the teacher – but never blame yourself. It's never your fault. But it's always your fault because if you wanted change, you're the one who has got to change."*
*KATHARINE HEPBURN*

*"I would not interfere with any creed of yours*
*Or want it to appear that I have all the cures.*
*There is so much to learn.*
*So many things are true.*
*The way my feet must go may not be right for you.*
*And so I give this spark*
*Of what is light to me*
*To guide you through the dark*
*But not to tell you what to see."*
*SPIRIT OF ANAC*

Well this has been one heck of a lesson in life.

I have learned so much that I know I will take forward with me and that will help me to continue to grow and develop.

I feel I have graduated with 'flying colours' (sorry I just had to get that in!) and I am very proud of myself.

I now see myself as a strong and courageous person who can take on whatever life puts my way and that if it feels right in my heart then I will rise to the challenge.

So – what are my key life lessons learned?

To put my health and happiness in front of everything else.

To always follow my heart. If it doesn't feel right, I can pretty much guarantee it isn't right.

Stand in my own truth – look into my heart. That is where the truth lies and I know I must be strong and courageous enough to 'stand' in that truth. Believe me, it feels good (even if it can be a little bit scary at times).

To stand by my values, however far it takes me out of my comfort zone and across the terror barrier. It is always best in the long run.

To surround myself with family and loved ones and people who share my values.

Continue to learn regarding the power of my mind. Whether it is the science or the spiritual (or a bit of both, like it has been for me), I have found an approach that is just right for me.

To relax! I have learned this is so vital to enable that smooth flow of positive energy around me. I do this through Reiki, meditation and being out in nature (you see...... I am a closet hippy tree hugger! There, I have finally admitted it because I am standing in my own truth!).

To go with the flow. I have learned not to fight against the natural ebb and flow of life and to just go with it. To know clearly where I am destined to go but to then let the Universe work its magic in terms of the 'how'. This book would not have happened unless I had learned to pick up on the hints and nudges that are presented to me from higher realms through my intuition and 'light bulb' moments.

Take responsibility. I have learned to take complete responsibility for EVERYTHING that has happened in my life. I have also learned that as soon as I did that, things started to get better.

Release and forgive. I have learned that it is very damaging to hold onto the past and harbour negative thoughts and emotions. It is so liberating to 'cleanse' all those worries away. I have learned to release it all and forgive myself and anyone who I feel has harmed me.

Not to be one of life's victim's - I have learned to look at negative situations in my life in a completely different way.

Not as the victim, but as the student. What life lesson did I learn from this?

To discover my inner child. To see the world through a fresh pair of untainted eyes. To laugh out loud; to sing like no one is listening and to dance like no one is watching!

To get on life's roller coaster and let out a massive scream of joy, anticipation and excitement as it sets off!

Now...this is the first.....the last.......the one and only time I am going to let Jon have the last word. Over to you Jon, and thanks for being my rock; for keeping me grounded and for being my soul mate on this fascinating journey.

---

## View from the Ground

I truly believe the words in this book are inspirational. How can I say that? Well, they are real and they are from the heart. I have lived this journey with Viv, and this is just the start of something incredibly special. It is wonderful that Viv has been given the opportunity to share her learnings with you and I truly hope you will be inspired in your own life.

I appreciate that some of Viv's spiritual words may not have fitted comfortably with everything you understand and believe but I hope in the context of the book, it has helped you to understand these are part of the overall experiences of an extraordinary ordinary person.

I am honoured to have been able to join Viv on her journey, and to have my mind opened to what is possible when having an open mind.

Do I talk to angels? No I don't.

Am I taken on journeys of learning when partaking in a Shamanic Meditation? No I am not?

Do I have a crystal that I can ask questions and it gives me answers? No, I don't.

But do I believe that Viv has these experiences? Yes I do, as she is blessed and gifted.

Why is she? Ask the universe.

As for the crystal, I have seen how this works. I will remember for a long time Viv shouting for me to come upstairs. Of course, I panicked but dutifully ran to her to see the crystal rocking backwards and forwards – completely unaided. Mad, but the power of the energy is incredible.

Before I close, I just need to clarify something. On that fateful day when we had our clear out and I managed to give up 12 ties, I did not have a yellow polka dot tie. I accept, the tie was yellow, it was patterned and the pattern included dots – but it was not polka dot!!

Anyway, I am proud to have been involved with Viv's book and I look forward to being able to contribute to future publications. As I have already said, I hope this provides you with the inspiration to take control of your life; be yourself; to love; be grateful, and do not let anyone tell you what to do; what to be or what to say.

Come on.....let's fly!

**Jon**

# My Children's Christmas Cards Say It All

*"There are only two lasting bequests we can hope to give our children. One of these is roots, the other....wings."*
*JOHANN WOLFGANG VON GOETHE*

We have developed this lovely tradition in our house. It has just happened naturally and is wonderful. Every year for Christmas and birthdays we write longer and longer messages in our cards to each other. The card messages are more precious to me than the presents.

It has got to be a bit of a competition between Ben and Livia as to who can make me cry the most!

Whilst it is a joke, I will never cease to feel so blessed that I have a 19 year old and 16 year old who put such heartfelt things in our cards.

Before I started writing this book, I knew that I would finish it with the children's messages because they are so powerful and just about encapsulate how far I have come and how others (even young teenagers!!) perceive this, and unlike a lot of the book which has changed organically as I have gone along, this Chapter remains exactly how I planned.

These are the Christmas cards I received three months ago from Ben and Livia.

## From Ben

"To Mum

I sometimes struggle to express this vocally, so prefer to write it down. The last few months have given me reflection time to realise just how much you mean to me. I always knew you were special, just not this special. The way you have dealt with 'X' inspired me to move on every time I have any small setback or hitches in the road. Every time I hear 'Angels' I think of you and I do truly think that is our song. Even though I'm away from home my heart always lies there and it always will.

Thank you for inspiring me. Keep smiling.

"Down the waterfall, wherever it may take me. I know that life won't break me."

Love Ben xxxxx"

## From Livia

As I dug this out from the box where I had saved the cards I couldn't help but smile when I noticed there was a cornflower blue ribbon tied around the card and tied in a butterfly bow at the front.

"Dear Mum

Merry Christmas

You're a hero. The amount of bravery you have shown this year is incredible. You have defied all odds and beaten every negative thing that has been thrown at you, even when they are life changing and so stressful.

You are so strong, so free willed and so noble. I want you never ever to forget that mum, no matter who tries to prove otherwise because they are ever so wrong.

You are achieving what you were put on earth to do and changing so many people's lives for the better.

You are the light, a beacon of hope to so many people.

I am so proud to call you my mother and if you sometimes need it, I will protect you and support you if ever you need it, to repay you for the amount of times you have saved me and others.

*Lots of love*

*Livviy*

*xxxxxx*

I sincerely hope you have enjoyed this book and it has helped you. I have heard some wonderful stories from people who have read the book and the positive impact it has had on them. You can share your own experiences of how the book has impacted you and join our 'uplifted spirits' community of people at

Facebook: www.facebook.com/pages/These-Wings-Can-Fly/
Twitter: @thsewingscanfly
Website: http://thesewingscanfly.wordpress.com/
Vivienne

**This book is a little gem!**
**Audrey Kirk**

*"Having read a number of other books of a similar genre, I found "These Wings Can Fly" to be a refreshing take on the theme of personal development. The book is inspiring and challenges convention; it combines the spiritual and the scientific, which makes it a fascinating and compelling read.*

*The book has two standout features which set it apart from others – the personal, genuine style of writing which demonstrates the author's honesty and humanity throughout; and the second voice part, which offers an alternative, more pragmatic view of the experience.*

*I found I could relate to many parts of the book, and especially loved the references to music lyrics as these really resonated with me; as well as the various quotes used throughout. "These Wings Can Fly" has inspired me to challenge myself and to open my mind further to the potential of the human mind. Powerful stuff!*

*I would definitely recommend this book to anyone who is interested in the human mind, personal development or who simply wishes to read an inspirational and honest book."*

**A beautifully written and thought provoking book**
**Steve Ramsden**

*"A beautifully written and thought provoking book. As someone who hadn't read a book from cover to cover for ages, when "These Wings Can Fly" was recommended to me I was certain it was going to be another of those books*

*I picked up and quickly got bored of. Not so....once into it, I found it very difficult to put down. I particularly like the "View from the ground" sections which give a real sense of Vivienne and Jon's journey. This book has certainly changed the way I look at life. Thank you!"*

## Miracles abound...
## Gwendolyn Plano

*"Vivienne writes as though she were a long lost friend, a loved one who is sharing her discoveries of the last years. This familiarity drew me into the book and gave extra credibility to the stories that unfolded. My unknown sister talked of the changes in her life as she began to see the blessings in life's challenges. Her gratitude reinforced my own and ultimately served as a reminder of life's true purpose. Interestingly, though we have never met and though our life circumstances are quite different, our realizations are the same. I marvel at the miracles of life—she being one."*

## A must read
## Karen Neame

*"Emotional, inspirational and life changing. This book made me cry as realisation dawned. A well written and often funny book that is believable. A life changer."*

## Fantastic Book , Great Author
## Ryan Askew

*"Wow every time I pick These Wings Can Fly up to read, I have a positive feeling that goes from my head to my toes. It's a truly amazing book with such a powerful concept. I'm so proud to be involved within the book. Great work Viv thanks for being a friend and helping me on the journey forward."*

## A powerful book of self-discovery and spiritual development
## Amanda Heenan

*"These Wings Can Fly is a book telling the story of awakening and self discovery, which gently encourages the reader to come along on the journey and make their own discoveries. The book includes a 'view from the ground' provided by the author's husband, which offers a pragmatic perspective as he observes his own and the author's path of spiritual growth and discovery. The book appeals on many different levels: the author's warm voice tells her story honestly, with a sense of wonder at what she discovers, and gently encourages the reader to put some universal principles into practice. There are some great practical exercises and meditations which I've put into practice with great effect. This is a great book for anyone interested in self and spiritual development."*

## Inspirational Read!
## Caroline Sheerin

*"An amazing book! Connected with so much! Couldn't put It down!! Found it a very positive energising read which has had a profound effect on me!"*

## Vivienne really will help you to fly!
## Dr. Barrie Hopson

*"And I suffer from vertigo! .....Vivienne is a 'one-off' in the best sense of the word, not least of which is her point with this book that anyone can embark on a personal journey like she does. Magically written with wonderful stories on how she slowly and painfully discovered her life purpose and even learning valuable lessons from the most distressing experiences and very difficult individuals."*

**Definite recommendation!**
**Abi Waller**

*"I have already read the whole book and have started reading again, this time participating in some 'finding yourself' exercises. I see this book as a form of catharsis. Whilst reading this book I felt sympathy, empathy, sadness, joy, relief and realisation and managed to release emotions I have been holding in for almost 2 years, since Granddad passed. It has really opened up my eyes to new explanations. It has also put into words some experiences, thoughts and feelings I have never been able to explain myself and the 'view from the ground' sections, a down-to-earth view on things, really make the book comical as well as realistic and believable. This is not just a book about spiritual experiences, it is a story. A fantastic story of an amazing couple and their journey of change, almost fictional it is so interesting, a fairy tale, but at the same time a non-fictional book, including scientific detail. I honestly don't know what more to say. It is unique and outstanding and completely worth the read! Give it a go."*

Lightning Source UK Ltd.
Milton Keynes UK
UKOW05f1942130714

235037UK00001B/24/P